3-Minute e-Learning

Rapid Learning and Applications,
Amazingly Lower Cost and Faster Speed
of Development

Plus 50 online demos, examples, templates, and
20 video vignettes

Ray Jimenez, Ph.D.

Monogatari

Library of Congress Cataloging-in-Publication Data

Library of Congress data has been applied for.

Monogatari Press

ISBN 978-0-9791847-0-3   0-9791847-0-3

Portions of this book first appeared in eLearning Guild e-Magazine Learning
Solutions.

How to Contact the Publisher

To order copies of this book in bulk, at a discount, call Monogatari Press
at 626-930-0160 or send email to support@vignettestraining.com.

To ask questions about the book, contact the author, or report a mistake in the text,
please write to Ray Jimenez, at rjimenez@vignettestraining.com

Online Examples and Resources

Note: To access a secure server and preview the examples, please
access http://vftlps.com/resources.

For **keynote presentations, consulting, workshops and 3-Minute content
development services**, please send email to Ray Jimenez at
rjimenez@vignettestraining.com.

To my real heroes

Marisu, Raymond, and Francesca

Acknowledgment

I am indebted to the hundreds of people who provided the inspiration and opportunities to test ideas, through their writings provoked me to ask questions and discover answers and for those who finally helped write this book. I cannot name them all here. Special recognition is due to a number of them. Ed Martin, Lance Dublin, Elliott Masie, Jay Cross, Richard Cross, Anthony Karrer, Ivan Cortes, Gary Van Antwerp, Ed Schneider, Judi Sharp, Teresita Vaquer, Maricel Sesdoyro, Cheryl Borsoto, Arn Reodique, Vikram Singh, Rafael Santo Tomas, Patrick Kehres, Debbie Glick, Chris Terrill, Bob Huebner, Maria Simpson, Bill Brandon, Michael Baroff, Joe DiDonato, Ann Buzzotta, Vic Buzzotta, Katherine Haynes, Susan Cole, Diane Allessi Williams, Eileen Dello-Martin, Jeffrey Groff, and Portia Groff and to my e-Learning associates and virtual team members in the Philippines, India, Canada, United Kingdom, Columbia and the United States of America.

My heartfelt thanks to Aramark, Cisco, American Bankers Association Education Foundation, Disney, Volvo Penta, U.S. Tennis Association, U.S. Government Accountability Office, Ryland Homes, Countrywide Home Loans, Nexans North America, U.S. Air Force, National Aeronautics and Space Administration (NASA), Psychological Associates, Inc., Monterey Consulting, Cognos Online, Oakwood Worldwide, Chipotle Mexican Grill, Virginia Credit Union, Dollar Tree Stores, Inc., Training Magazine Events and eLearning Guild.

If you want to know ...

How to cut development costs down to 30%, turn to page   181

Interview techniques to help Subject Matter Experts (SME), check out   C-3

Create performance driven content, go to page   B-12

Add performance metrics in your LMSs, see page   167

Layout content into small lessons or snippets, check out page   B-34

Estimating costs and production timelines, go to page   B-55

Access live and online demos, templates and examples,
visit www.vignettestraining.com

Contents

ix

3-Minute e-Learning
Introduction

3-Minute e-Learning Introduction

The purchase of YouTube by Google for $1.6 billion reminds us that a great many people in mainstream society access, share, collaborate, and learn from each other at faster speeds, with highly personalized experiences, and a lot of independence. This is the new world of Web 2.0 – social computing or social networking.

On the surface, it may seem ludicrous to correlate classroom training and e-Learning with YouTube joining Google. However, there are many indications that the very foundations of how we train people today are being significantly influenced or altered by the same behaviors and technologies that Google and YouTube cultivate. These two symbols of social computing and social networking have a profound impact on training and learning.

The challenge to leaders, trainers, instructional designers and developers continues to be: "How do we add value while we leverage rapidly changing technologies and modify our approaches to match new social computing behaviors?"

Addressing this question compels us to wrestle with the nuts and bolts of e-Learning: content development and delivery. How do we define and approach content as we deliver it through high speed Internet tools and in the world of Web 2.0? How do we develop content that suits the new learning and work behaviors of people in electronically connected workplaces?

e-Learning landscape changes: e-Learning 2.0, "working and full proficiencies"

The e-Learning landscape has changed. In our study of content development and delivery, two related changes provide insights that address the fundamental shifts.

First, web 2.0 and social networking tools have invaded the e-Learning field with tools, such as WIKIs, blogs, Federated Searches, Podcasts, RSS and other similar ones. Anthony Karrer, Ph.D., a leading expert in e-Learning systems development (www.techempower.com.com), speaks of e-Learning 2.0, as opposed to e-Learning 1.0 and e-Learning 1.3. (Please see Table 0-1). Karrer suggests that as the approach moves into e-Learning 2.0, the content is reduced from 60 minutes in e-Learning 1.0 to 15 minutes in e-Learning 1.3 and just one minute in e-Learning 2.0.

The one minute of content in e-Learning 2.0 is provided by the worker or learner, whereas the content in e-Learning 1.0 is provided by instructional designers and trainers. In addition to WIKIs, blogs, searches, Podcasts, and RSS, learners contribute their own experiences and expertise-making content development – a collaborative process of the learners.

Karrer further suggests that e-Learning 2.0 does not replace e-Learning 1.0 or e-Learning 1.3, but, instead, provides new options in the already large array of e-Learning tools. Moreover, under the right conditions, implementing e-Learning 2.0 is a compelling option.

	e-Learning 1.0	e-Learning 1.3	e-Learning 2.0
Main Components	Courseware, authoring tool, LMS	Reference hybrids, LCMS, discussion groups	Wiki, social networking, bookmarking, add-ins, mash-ups
Ownership	Top-down, one-way	Top-down, some collaborative	Bottom-up, learner-driven, peer learning
Development time	Long	Rapid	None
Content size	60 minutes	15 minute	1 minute
Access time	Prior to work	In between work	During work
Delivery	At one time	In many pieces	When you need it
Content access	LMS	Email, intranet	Search, RSS feed
Driver	ID	Learner	Worker
Content creator	ID	SME	Worker

 Figure 0-1: e-Learning 2.0

This table is provided with permission from Anthony Karrer, Ph.D. (www.techempower.com.com).

Second, in another development, at the Workforce Performance 2006 conference on September 11, 2006, Joe DiDonato, EVP - Chief Learning Technologies Officer for Countrywide Home Loans, Inc., presented his observations on the need to differentiate "working proficiency" from "full proficiency." DiDonato explained:

"Given the tasks of training an individual to 'full proficiency' in a technical product, the education teams (instructional designers, trainers, developers) will do a complete decomposition of that product, and then proceed to train an employee on those product functions. This ritual of 'full proficiency' training ignores the fact that much of this knowledge will probably never be used that is frequently in the employee's job, and in a lot of cases, simply forgotten once the employee leaves the classroom."

Instead of full proficiency, DiDonato suggested focusing on "working proficiency," that is, providing information that an employee needs to do the job immediately and most of the time. This distinction aids in deciding what tools are best suited to deliver the different levels of content.

Furthermore, DiDonato concluded that the classroom model is not an efficient model for dealing with the volume of information that needs to be processed in today's organizations. He offered a mixture of solutions to reduce the time required to achieve "working proficiency." DiDonato included classroom training as a tool to help in building skills to achieve "working proficiency." However, he suggested that perhaps 80% of content can be accessed by learners through Federated Searches and wizards.

Performance-driven content versus boring content, bordering

on really "crappy" content

Amidst these new shifts and developments, there is one remaining truth that will stay with us for a long while. Regardless of the technologies and the different ways people behave and learn, we still have to create, organize and deliver content. In businesses and nonprofit organizations, where content is in the fabric of their culture, the demand is even greater for rapid, small, and useful content. Both Karrer and DiDonato recognize the difficulties of organizing and making content available to learners rapidly, and they present technologies that may help to access them faster. e-Learning 2.0 broadens our suite of technologies, while the concept of "working proficiency" helps us to focus our content on performance.

e-Learning 2.0 broadens our suite of technologies, while the concept of "working proficiency" helps us to focus our content on

The challenge with the Web 2.0 social networking and computing environment is that it is unstructured, promotes independence and empowers everyone to publish content, good or bad, useful or crappy. In our organizations, however, we need to provide content that has productive value to our workers. And productive value means useful content presented in a way that decreases the time needed for learning. Whether we apply e-Learning 2.0 tools, e-Learning 1.0 or 1.3, it is apparent that the technologies promote learning behaviors that operate in a rapid, need-to-know, and just-in-time environment.

What we see today in many e-Learning programs ranges from boring to really crappy content. With Web 2.0 and advances in digital and authoring tools, the content created only 3-5 years ago may become crappy very quickly, not because of visual quality and aesthetics, but because of its inability to provide learners with the content they need instantly to perform at work.

3-Minute e-Learning – rapid application, rapid development and rapid delivery

3-Minute e-Learning is not just a figurative title, but a practical yardstick.

In 3-Minute e-Learning, the basic structure of a learning snippet, nugget, lesson or vignette provides the compelling context (through a story, example, or case), key ideas, key applications and optional access to reference or detailed information. Learners study or access 3-Minute e-Learning and spend literally about three minutes with it.

The core of 3-Minute e-Learning is the encapsulation of "application points" or performance ideas, what DiDonato calls "working proficiency" knowledge. The "application points" are those segments of knowledge that enable the learner to apply the ideas to an actual work-related problem or situation rapidly. In essence, 3-Minute e-Learning is meant to help learners use knowledge instantly!

Incidentally, I am not suggesting that eight-hour classroom training should be reduced to 3-Minute e-Learning. Rather, that the "application points" or

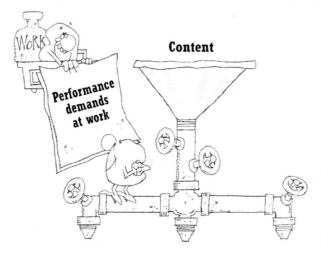

3-Minute e-Learning

"working proficiency" knowledge is the core content presented in 3-Minute e-Learning.

Key shifts in thinking needed

Three fundamental thought processes must change to accomplish 3-Minute e-Learning:

1. Creating 3-Minute e-Learning is not about finding the software that produces content most rapidly. It is about rethinking and focusing on how to isolate the "application points" in the most bloated content and apply the step-by-step process of developing 3-Minute e-Learning to those "application points."

2. It is only by going to the roots of performance outcomes, expectations and realities that we can identify the crucial "application points." 3-Minute e-Learning cannot be developed based on a job description, duties and responsibilities or task analysis.

3. Selecting Rapid e-Learning development software, authoring tools or an LMS will be easier, less costly, and more effective when we have taken into account items 1 and 2 above. Embracing a rapid development tool without defining the "application points" will not meet the goals of 3-Minute e-Learning, Rapid e-Learning and rapid application.

The benefits of 3-Minute e-Learning, rapid application and rapid development

3-Minute e-Learning helps us simplify our Rapid e-Learning efforts. It will increase our ability to add value to our organization by demonstrating lower production costs and faster development results.

1. 3-Minute e-Learning increases the speed with which learners apply the ideas, thereby impacting performance. This helps us add value to our organization's needs.

2. We can position 3-Minute e-Learning not just as a course or a program, but as an immediate problem solving tool, for example, to help technicians in the field, cashiers in stores, managers who need to learn about specific skills, and salespeople who need updates on product changes. If we make the content too large or too bulky, we will lose this opportunity. Please see Appendix B.

3. 3-Minute e-Learning provides a clearly-defined process for working successfully with Subject Matter Experts (SMEs). The process, which is contained in a series of interview questions in Appendix C, helps us direct the contributions of SMEs to a focused 3-Minute e-Learning snippet, nugget or vignette.

4. 3-Minute e-Learning reduces costs and increases productivity. With this methodology, as I will demonstrate in this book, we can reduce our development costs by 50% and increase the speed of development by 300%. In actual dollars, this means that a program built in a traditional fashion costing $50,000, will cost only $20,000 using the 3-Minute e-Learning process, a savings of at least 60%. Please see Chapter 22.

5. One of the unintended consequences of 3-Minute e-Learning is that our content will be useful in the world of rapidly, random and self-directed

learning, especially in Web 2.0 applications. 3-Minute e-Learning makes our content flexible, versatile and useful at three levels: e-Learning 1.0, 1.3 and 2.0. It will find its value in Knowledge Management Systems, Learning Management Systems, and virtual online tools such as WebEx or Breeze. It can also work well as a reference and searchable format.

With 3-Minute e-Learning as foundation of the content delivery, we enable the leaners to search, bookmark and send email. Furthermore, we will be able to correlate e-Learning with performance metrics. This helps us see the impact of training in actual job performance. Please see Chapter 21.

Relationship of 3-Minute e-Learning and Rapid e-Learning

In this book I use the terms 3-Minute e-Learning and Rapid e-Learning interchangeably. The distinction, however is, 3-Minute e-Learning is the outcome while Rapid e-Learning is the process of accomplishing the outcome.

3-Minute e-Learning and the pathways

For the past few years, I have worked and advised many leaders in organizations on "how to produce content into small pieces." I have also been involved in designing and implementing Learning Management Systems (LMS) to enhance their capacities to impact measurable performance. There seems to be a growing dissatisfaction with the first generation of e-Learning content and LMSs – classroom-like lessons and page turning, and the massive use of multimedia, simulation, interactivity and tracking – that needs to be addressed. 3-Minute e-Learning addresses that dissatisfaction.

Regardless of what we now do in e-Learning, 3-Minute e-Learning will help us take an honest look at how we can propel our e-Learning initiatives into a new e-Learning landscape, one that is inching faster and faster into our workplaces, faster than we can retool, reorganize and redesign.

3-Minute e-Learning provides the pathways in that landscape.

Why Are We Going "Gaga"?

Chapter 1

Why Are We Going "Gaga"?

To develop 3-Minute e-Learning, there is a need to apply Rapid e-Learning. Rapid e-Learning as a term is redundant. By definition, e-Learning is already rapid. Its principles are all about speed – and quality as well. It provides immediate, personalized learning at its best, and its tools and software are fast, inexpensive and have more capabilities than we can ever imagine using.

So why are we going "gaga" over Rapid e-Learning design and development? I suspect that the training industry – trainers, managers, designers, developers, suppliers and everyone else – has come to realize that many of the e-Learning programs are not making the mark. e-Trainers, developers and managers are failing to live up to or deliver the dream and promise of e-Learning.

This is both good news and bad news. The good news is that there is a strong desire to make e-Learning work. The bad news is that we jump too fast to adopt rapid development without really thinking through the desired outcomes and the appropriate processes. Instead of using Rapid e-Learning to produce 3-Minute e-Learning, we apply Rapid e-Learning to produce, faster and cheaper, linear and classroom-like e-Learning programs. We are developing, cheaper and faster - the wrong outcomes.

Instead of saying, "We can do this better, cheaper and faster," we use the term "rapid" to call attention to the problem and add a sense of urgency. In this regard, I totally subscribe to the use of "rapid." However, to make Rapid e-Learning work, we need to focus on "significant" innovations – concepts, ideas, and models, and not just technology — that will actually make a huge difference in the quality, speed and costs. I propose we focus on 3-Minute e-Learning. But for heavens sake, let's focus on the *donut* and not the hole. Enough with the hype... let's go to work!

My proposition is that, if we understand and practice the sound fundamentals of e-Learning, our sharpened skills will enable us to produce 3-Minute e-Learning. We have been accustomed too long to develop many of our current e-Learning programs with one foot on the accelerator but with the other pressing hard on the brakes. When we let go of the brakes now, given then tips and techniques from this book, we will accelerate . . . rapidly, meaning, create 3-Minute e-Learning

that will raise performance on the job.

In this book, I will show that e-Learning inherently provides rapid learning and application. It offers the processes and tools that can accelerate, or rapidly push, e-Learning development. Specifically, you'll find ideas and tools to help you:

- Develop an e-Learning Architecture (e-LA) as a framework for rapid design and 3-Minute e-Learning
- Design the e-LA to meet business goals
- Use the e-LA to manage the content and design process
- Manage Subject Matter Experts, producers and software developers, IT staff, and management
- Find ways to speed up course development

with software and developers

- Cut the costs at each stage of the process
- Quantify your Rapid e-Learning design

e-Learning Project Development Flow

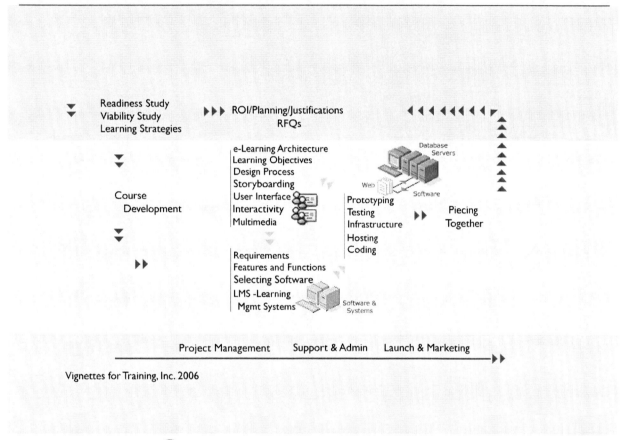

Vignettes for Training, Inc. 2006

Figure 1-1: e-Learning Project Development Flow

and development process

I will present an overview of the content design and development of the e-Learning development process. (See Figure 1-1 below)

Within this overview, I will critique a lot of today's e-Learning programs which are often built on inappropriate models of learning and outdated methods of instructional system design. I'll offer a tool to help you make basic decisions about strategies and tactics, and I'll introduce the concept of an e-LA.

Revolutionary and Incremental Solutions

Chapter 2

Revolutionary and Incremental Solutions

Through my work and experience, I have come to understand a number of issues that hold us back from using e-Learning or producing 3-Minute e-Learning effectively. I would like to share this perspective with you.

First, e-Learning development is often slow because we have yet to apply a fundamentally different way of designing learning programs for e-Learning (an e-Learning Architecture). Our learning design for e-Learners' needs is based on classroom-like conditions and not on new realities of fast-paced and rapidly changing business conditions. It still looks like we are designing programs based on 100-year-old assumptions about the way people learn, and about the way to design learning.

Second, many e-Learning programs are bloated with content, lectures, simulations, exercises – methods of forcing content and controlling the learner – which have minimal impact on the e-learners' needs (e-Learning Behaviors®) for quick access, solutions and applications.

e-Learning programs are (1) often at least 50% heavier (too much content) and (2) at least 75% more cumbersome (too many controls) than e-Learners

I maintain that our e-Learning programs are (1) often at least 50% heavier (too much content) and (2) at least 75% more cumbersome (too many controls) than e-Learners require. If you want serious savings in costs and increasing speed of development, these two areas should be your focus in implementing revolutionary and incremental solutions.

This leads to my final observation: most e-Learning suffers from a poorly conceived architecture. A poorly conceived e-Learning Architecture (e-LA) means we have no way to manage the e-Learning design and development process. We fault subject matter experts (SMEs), developers, programmers, and software providers for a slow response. It should be the other way around: We need to present an architectural plan or infrastructure so that all the contributors to our e-Learning program can follow a streamlined process.

What can be done about these issues? There are a number of steps to take in addition to the ones mentioned above.

The first step is to recognize that **there are two important and parallel areas of focus to produce better, cheaper, and faster e-Learning programs (rapid development): the learning side and business side**. The learning side is about design, development, implementation and assessment. The business side is about quality, speed, cost, ease of use and value. Each side has a measurement standard. If we want to manage results, we can do so by implementing the **Organic e-Learning Design Principle** and using the **Rapid e-Learning Calculator.** I will explain these later.

SMEs are content experts, not e-Learning designers. Yet, we need SMEs to buy into our e-Learning Architecture so we can speed up the process and control the quality. (See Appendix C for the SME Discovery Process).

We are tempted to purchase and use software that doesn't have an e-LA. So, we spin our wheels asking what the software can do to speed up the process and improve quality. Unfortunately, the software does not do this. It is the "creative process" of the e-Learning Architecture that should dictate this, not the software. Remember "Garbage in, garbage out"? We can take it a step further: "The more garbage, the slower the speed and higher the costs – and the quality stinks!"

Software selection (authoring tools, platforms, Learning Management Systems) should support the learning and business standards. Lots of software is capable of providing 10,000% more than our actual needs, or even more than what we can use. Selecting the right software, or a combination of software, for our e-LA is both a learning design decision and business decision. Without a clear e-LA with learning and business standards, we either pick over-simplistic software or *software on steroids.* In other words, software is either overly-simplistic or souped-up depending on how it matches up to what we need. Quality is sacrificed, the speed of development is decreased, and the total costs are high when there is a mismatch between the software and the learning and business standards.

It is important to keep in mind that software developers and suppliers have their own "religions" based on a mixture of their backgrounds, interests and skill sets. Understanding these biases enables designers and developers to leverage the part of the software that works, to speed up development and cut costs. Knowing these biases also helps us ask whether there is a fit between the software and our actual need, skill set, budget and culture.

The decision to implement reusable tools, templates and applications is driven by a business purpose. Designers need to drive this purpose to maximize the input of software developers. Most producers are not software developers and know little about the capability for developing reusable utilities. We need to challenge software developers to provide a plan for reusability.

Adding interactivity, first and foremost, must be an e-LA decision, not a software decision. If you follow the software route first, we can slow down our process. Selecting what and how to implement interactivity is important to the quality of the program, but it is a delicate balance between the creative and software process. If thought out well, interactivity can be developed successfully even with the
least-capable software.

To increase the speed of development, use a collaboration process and tool. Introduce a culture change and process change to the SMEs, trainers, designers, developers, IT systems administrators, participants, managers and champions. Manage version controls, the change-order process, project timelines and tools. Use collaborative Internet real-time supported tools and software.

There are programs and organizations that are not prepared for rapid development. Certain cultural and structural barriers must be challenged before we can accomplish rapid development. We must know how to select the programs that create the most impact and can be rapidly deployed.

Whether or not improving value, cost and speed of the e-Learning design and development are worth all the effort is determined by how much the business gains from this activity. The closer we can link and connect business outcomes, either anecdotal or quantitative, the better we can justify the investment in Rapid e-Learning development.

A big factor in its favor is that Rapid e-Learning is in high demand. So, find out what the gains are, and the cost of rapid development can be justified. Simply comparing Rapid e-Learning development with other approaches is not a strong

3-Minute e-Learning Is Rapid Learning, Faster Application and Lower Cost

Chapter 3

3-Minute e-Learning Is Rapid Learning, Faster Application and Lower Cost

3-Minute e-Learning design and development means constructing e-Learning programs that **provide learners the opportunity to quickly apply knowledge to perform tasks and enable managers to make this happen.** It also means constructing such programs faster and cheaper to meet changing and demanding business conditions.

3-Minute e-Learning is the outcome of Rapid e-Learning. Rapid e-Learning design and development must also mean, "to lead to faster application" (whether this is learning, traditionally defined, or not). This is a requisite expectation; otherwise, we quickly find ourselves developing e-Learning programs for the

We can't rapidly write a novel; but we may rapidly write a check list or a quick help book.

wrong reasons. We must understand Rapid e-Learning development as much for its potential to create quality outcomes, as for its promises of speed and lower cost.

Learning outcomes - quality

Quality concerns refer to the learning outcomes. They show us how 3-Minute e-Learning helps the learners or workers perform the required tasks rapidly.

The focus is **"applying knowledge rapidly,"** not learning as traditionally de-

We are not defining learning outcomes as retention, completion, coverage, certification or performance of some tasks while in the e-Learning process. Here, we define learning outcomes on the basis of how fast and how easily a learner is able to apply knowledge and skill to given tasks.

fined.

Cheaper and faster development – gains and costs

The business drivers for Rapid e-Learning design and development must include the speed and cost of completion. Speed is a function of cost. The faster the development, the lower the cost must be; otherwise, greater speed may not warrant the incurred costs to produce the programs.

The overriding business reason is the *gain*. How will Rapid e-Learning design and development impact the business outcomes? Will it drive business costs down? Will it increase sales and cash flow, hasten early adoption or avoid penalties from government agencies? Will it help strengthen a strategic position?

*I have the suspicion that top management's impatience with slow e-Learning development is rooted in e-Learning's supposed inability to contribute to business performance. Although
e-Learning helps reduce the costs, it has yet to document its capability to add new value to business results.*

Anomaly in expectations

There is a pressure to focus on how to speed up development and cut the costs, but we pay less attention to whether programs will actually work. We are able to hype about the promise of e-Learning as faster and cheaper to deliver, but we are less able to justify the need for more time and resources to do a good job.

There is a risk that rapid development will create false expectations – a backlash that will haunt us as professionals and as an industry.

Rapid e-Learning Design and Development Models - Application Points and The Calculator

Chapter 4

Rapid e-Learning Design and Development Models - Application Points and The Calculator

As gleaned from the previous chapters, we are faced with the challenge to introduce a culture change and process change in e-Learning. Who are our major players in this endeavor? SMEs, trainers, designers, developers, IT systems administrators, participants, managers and champions. Organizations that are not yet prepared for and not confident enough to adopt 3-Minute e-Learning development need the major players and "heroes" to support the initiatives. A lot depends on these "heroes" to break through or totally demolish the cultural and structural barriers that get in the way of any organization's or business' goal to invest in Rapid e-Learning that gives the best outcomes.

Organic e-Learning Design Principle

Where do we think our major players will and should begin? Our best and most practical answer is: With the redefinition and clearer understanding of the Basic Principle of Organic e-Learning Design. This is preparatory to the actual design process that is covered in Chapter 8 of this book.

The Basic Principle of Organic e-Learning Design is a paradoxical paradigm shift.

Conventional thinking says that effective training is costly and it takes time to develop. The opposite is true in Organic e-Learning Design Process - "Faster is actually better and cheaper."

By focusing on the 20% content that allows e-learners to apply ideas instantly and get results quickly, two dramatic benefits materialize - the cost is down to 70% and the speed of development is 300% faster. It improves the quality and value of learning and application and the approach of development.

Traditionally, all training content is treated equally. Let's use a rectangular block to represent a solid body of content.

This is what different people have been saying to explain the block of content:

SMEs: "All content is important."

Instructional designers: "Learners have to learn based on competencies and learning objectives."

Trainers: "We'll train you in all of the content, just in case you need it."

Developers: "Let's present the content in colorful, engaging, and interactive slideshow."

Learners: "I scan, choose, and pick what I can use."

This statement from the last group of people, oftentimes, indicates that the interest of the learners is different from that of SMEs, instructional designers, trainers and developers. This is true whether they are in the classroom, reading a manual, attending online learning or virtual classroom session.

Learners look at content like pyramids with points.

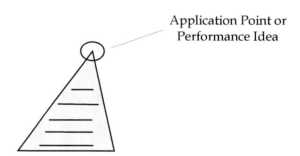

They pay attention to "application points". This means that instead of looking at a block of content, they look for key ideas in the content that they can apply and benefit by using immediately. They focus on what is relevant and what they can use. If the block of content is large with many sections or parts, the learners focus on the tips or points of the micro content. The tip of the micro content should contain the ideas that help them in their work, the "application points", or, we may say performance ideas.

In Rapid e-Learning, "application points" or performance ideas, which are quickly used at work, are essential. It is only when "application points" are easily identified and accessible that learners can learn in 3 minutes and achieve results quickly. In essence, this is the highest form of learning quality and value. It would serve us well, indeed, to remember that presenting the content as a block, using our symbol, stops the learner from having quick access to "application points" or performance ideas. The learner has less value or use for this type of content presentation. A block of content is just not conducive to rapid e-learning and application, much less 3-Minute e-Learning.

A block of content is disappointingly bloated, heavy, and long; not to mention uninteresting and boring. The greatest disadvantage is the high cost and slow pace of converting a block of content into e-Learning program. This activity, if pursued stubbornly or unknowingly, is a catastrophe in the making, for the following reasons.

A catastrophe in the making

First, let's say content from a classroom is converted to e-Learning using traditional approaches. It is linear and similar to a lecture.

Linear

Learners are clicking pages. "There is no way for me to choose, select, and find important information quickly. I have to go through all these pages", the learner complains.

Second, since clicking pages is really boring and hard for the learner to use, the

31

next "Aha" is "Let's make a video or slideshow."

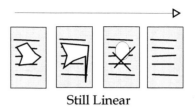

Still Linear

◁ Back Stop Forward ▷

"Kinda cool and graphical", says the learner. But it still takes long to produce and is not easy for the learner to learn from and perform and achieve results quickly.

Third, a more daring move is presented : "Let's use games, simulation, and interactivities."

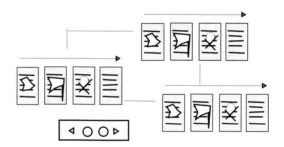

"Now, this is really entertaining!" the learner says. But it is even more difficult to apply the ideas quickly.

Fourth, "So that it is even quicker, let's use virtual learning tool, like WebEx or Interwise", says the trainer.

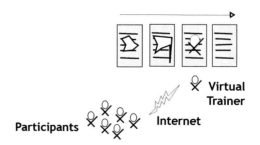

This approach is faster and convenient for the trainer, but not really helping the learner apply ideas any faster.

The catastrophe in all the above attempts is that it is it harder for the learner

to find promptly the "application points". It becomes frustrating because the usage of the program becomes limited or the learners do not get to complete the programs. The cost continues to grow and yet the development remains slow.

Incidentally, more multimedia and interactivity is not the answer. Without a new way of thinking about the content, multimedia and interactivity weaken most
e-Learning programs because they add to the heavy weight and bloated content.

Instant access to "Application Points"

The learner wants to view the content in this manner. The "application points" are instantly accessible so the learner can, in 3 minutes, internalize the knowledge and apply instantly the ideas and knowledge on the job.

"Application Points" Pyramids

How does the Organic e-Learning Design Principle impact Rapid e-Learning? As mentioned earlier, Rapid e-Learning is designed to enable the learner to understand and learn in 3 minutes, and quickly and confidently apply ideas and knowledge to perform tasks. Furthermore, Rapid e-Learning reduces the costs and increases the speed of development.

To accomplish the desired results for Rapid e-Learning, we need to apply the 3-Minute e-Learning and Organic e-Learning Design Principles in our e-Learning projects.

Here are helpful tips to answer these questions:

How to successfully identify the "application points" or performance ideas?

How to strip content of its bloat and heavy weight?

How to select or use software applications to support the learner's need to identify and use "application points"?

Finally, how to use a Rapid e-Learning development process that accomplishes the above results at the lowest cost and the fastest speed possible?

Appendix B provides an extensive process to facilitate the accomplishment of these goals.

The Rapid e-Learning Calculator

To successfully implement a 3-Minute Rapid e-Learning development plan, we need to use a yardstick or set standards that can compare the savings in time and costs, and can also ensure quality. This yardstick, the Rapid e-Learning Calculator (see Table 4.1), has been designed to assess strategies and tactics. Based on our assessment, we can decide if the approach is worth the effort and if it pays off.

One of the purposes of the Rapid e-Learning Calculator is to cover not only the quantitative areas of our study but also the qualitative considerations. There may be quantitative outcomes in speed and time savings, but these may not make sense in qualitative terms.

For example, a particular authoring tool might be inexpensive to acquire (a quantitative measure), but what if it is hard to use and the software support is unresponsive (the qualitative downside)? Or, suppose the software is inflexible. Could it hamper our ability to introduce creative ideas and solutions?

There is a trade-off between outcomes in the above example. We always need to find ways to balance the quantitative and qualitative outcomes according to a number of criteria. Here are the standards and some factors to consider:

- **Quality**
  - o Value to learners, immediate application, engagement, access, and speed of learning
  - o Aesthetic value and experience

- **Time/Speed**
    - o Short distance from concept to delivery, time lapsed – chronological calendar
    - o Value of response to business need to be the first to market
    - o Avoidance of costs or lost opportunity; gains by meeting timelines; reducing downtime, waiting time, and/or wasted time

- **Cost in hours**
    - o Cost per output
    - o Maximized use of talent
    - o Learning cost
    - o Administrative costs

TABLE 4.1: Rapid e-Learning calculator					
Rate from 1 (low) to 5 (high) the value of each strategy or tactic in Rapid e-Learning development.	1	2	3	4	5
I **Rapid e-Learning Generator:** *(In the section studied, write in this box what potentially can help you in rapid development).*					
II **Rapid e-Learning Standards** (Assess the generator 1=low, 5=high)					
1 **Quality:** Value to learners, immediate applications,engagement,accessibility and speed, speed of learning; Aesthetic value and experience					
2 **Time/Speed:** Cycle from concept to delivery, time lapse- calendar: Response value to business time needs; Avoidance of costs or opportuninty lost; Meeting timelines; Reducing downtime, waiting time, wasted time; Time-to-market					
3 **Cost in hours:** Cost per output; Best use of talent; Learning cost; Price					
4 **Ease/difficulty:** Efficient process, least effort to get results; Low frustration factor					
5 **Value contribution:** Impact on operations, increasing revenues, profits and cash flow, reduction cost, competitiveness, returns to stakeholders; Quantifies returns - anecdotal or factual; Speed of being ahead of competition; Breakthrough innovation (significant) or incremental change (marginal)					
III **My Action Plan:** (Write how you will implement the likely gains.)					

- **Ease/Difficulty**
  - o Efficient process, least effort to get results
  - o Low frustration factor

- **Value contribution**
  - o Impact on operations, increasing revenues, profits, and cash flow, cost reduction, competitiveness, returns to stakeholders; quantified returns – anecdotal or statistical
  - o Speed of being ahead of competition
  - o Breakthrough innovation (significant) or incremental change (marginal)

The key rule to remember is:
Make change where it matters. Implement solutions that are breakthrough innovations before you apply tactical or incremental innovations.

Rapid e-Learning critical areas for review

In any e-Learning project, there are areas or points within the flow of development where it pays to review the standards. It helps to ask: what is the impact of each possible method or strategy on Rapid e-Learning? Looking back at the Project Development Flow, in Figure 1-1, these six areas are critical in finding opportunities for Rapid e-Learning:

- Learning design
- Content development
- Software selection
- Development process
- Implementation
- Assessment

The Rapid e-Learning Calculator

To proceed in developing and implementing rapid development strategies and tactics, we need to know which approach in each of these critical areas is "worth the effort." It is easy to adopt small, tactical changes that have very little impact on the overall rapid deployment of your project.

Admittedly, the accumulation of incremental innovations (small changes) can
mean significant savings in time and cost. However, being overwhelmed with small improvements and not having the time or energy to focus on major innovations could wreck our Rapid e-Learning initiatives. The Rapid e-Learning Calculator can help us identify and make change where it mat-

ters.

How the Rapid e-Learning Calculator works and how to use it

The Rapid e-Learning Calculator is a tool we can use to evaluate the ideas that we will read about in this book and to decide how we might apply them. In other words, let us pause periodically and review how the ideas can have impact on our work or projects. We use the Calculator, pick the relevant areas, categorize the impact from 1 (low) to 5 (high), and note our conclusions in the area provided for action planning.

The key principle is this: solutions (which may be ideas, processes, methods, alternative strategies, or software tools) are *generators* (Rapid e-Learning generators). They create some level of change to meet the *rapid standards*. Assess the generator based on the standards. (We can also use the Calculator to compare two alternatives.) Then, write the gains and implementation in *My Action Plan*. (Refer to this section in Table 4.1: Rapid e-Learning Calculator).

The goal is to be able to prioritize those generators that are of value to us, especially those that we can implement right away for immediate returns.

Our action plan must be realistic, clear, concise and very specific. We must also assign people, budget and timelines to the plan. Show me the money!

e-Learning Architecture (e-LA)- Foundation for Rapid e-Learning

Chapter  5

e-Learning Architecture (e-LA)- Foundation for Rapid e-Learning

An e-Learning Architecture (e-LA) is a learning framework that meets the needs of e-learners and the demands of the business or organization. It consists of philosophies, methodologies and processes to deliver the e-Learning programs effectively, inexpensively and rapidly.

Many e-Learning programs rest on shaky learning foundations and structures. Their learning architecture is ill-conceived or non-existent. Most of the processes and frameworks are borrowed from old models and old assumptions in training. Examples of these models and assumptions include classic Instructional Systems Design (ISD) models, "talking head" media, and other teacher-driven or expert-driven approaches. Many developers fail to follow an e-LA on which they can build their design and development processes. Progress in this area has been slow in many organizations.

e-Learning Architecture provides clarity of standards, and streamlined decision making and learning outcomes.

The lack of a sound instructional architecture for e-Learning is one key reason for the slow and costly development in e-Learning. Furthermore, it impacts negatively on the quality of e-Learning programs.

This e-Learning Architecture provides clear directions for design, processes, software and resource requirements - leading to clarity of standards, streamlined decision making and balance between business and learner needs.

We face four challenges:

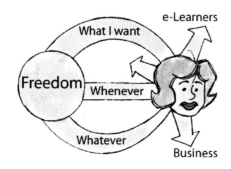

- *What e-LA meets our rapid business needs?*

- *What learning architecture works best for quality e-Learning programs?*

- *What process can support this architecture?*

- *How do we develop content that follows this architecture?*

The three core issues are:

- *e-Learning instructional design*

- *Content development*

- *Design process*

"Flexible and nimble instructional design"

A survey conducted by The eLearning Guild and presented by Joe Pulichino highlights several related areas that are affected by the need for an e-Learning Architecture. The study took place in February, 2005 for the members and friends of The eLearning Guild. (Please see "The Rapid e-Learning Development Research Report" in Appendix A. I will only cite two of the questions here.)

The responses to question 16 in the survey (see Figure 5-1 on the next page) show that the top three key areas to rapid instructional design are infrastructure, innovation in instructional design and improvement in content management.

Pulichino comments:

"Traditional instruction design models will either have to be set aside and replaced, or updated to make them more flexible and nimble in light with the demands on e-Learning."

> **Q16.** In your opinion, what are the three keys to rapid instructional design for e-Learning content: (Select only three.)
>
> 77% Infrastructure to support rapid design (technology, etc.)
>
> 60% Innovation in instructional design strategies
>
> 40% Improved content management and use of LCMSs
>
> 40% Concurrent phases of instructional design process
>
> 23% Reduction of some phases of intructional design process
>
> 15% Working faster
>
> 9% Outsourcing of some phases of instructional design process
>
> 8% Other
>
> 2% I do not know
>
> 0% 10% 20% 30% 40% 50% 60% 70% 80% 90% 100%
>
> For this question we asked respondents to select the three most important keys to rapid e-Learning design. The clear leader is "infrastructure to support rapid design" (77%). Certainly, a process can move no more quickly that its slowest point, so to enable a rapid process we need to have a complete infrastructure that can help speed the process up, such as available templates to serve as starting points. The fact that innovation is instructional design strategies also had a high response percentage indicates that traditional instructional design models will either have to be set aside and replaced, or updated to make them more flexible and nimble in light of the "demands" of rapid e-Learning.

 Figure 5-1: *Responses to Question 16*

Setting aside or updating traditional instructional models is essential for Rapid e-Learning development. The change has to occur because the age-old models in designing programs don't apply to e-Learning design. Without an innovation in e-Learning Architecture, there is no mold from which to pattern our design and processes, or for the proper selection and use of software.

According to Josh Bersin of Bersin & Associates, a leading e-Learning research firm, these models or methods follow the "waterfall approach", which takes too long:

> *"Today's e-Learning programs are being developed with the waterfall approach. An SME explains the content; an instructional designer creates a design document and project plan; a web-developer builds interactivities and HTML pages; a QA engineer tests the course; and then a few months later, an online course is launched.*
>
> *Although this approach is proven and works well, it breaks down from many time-critical problems. It demands a team of skilled*

*professionals and it can take months to complete …. this waterfall
process simply takes too long and costs too much for many business*

*situations. Oftentimes the business problem has changed during the
development of the course!"*

Rapid – but must meet e-learners needs', e-Learning behaviors

A second and more important issue to confront is that using traditional instructional models forces the e-Learning design to be "school-like" or "classroom-like." These types of programs tend to talk down to, lecture to and control the learner.

Dr. Sivasailam "Thiagi" Thiagarajan, president of Workshops by Thiagi, Inc., summarizes his views about what's wrong:

*"The whole ISD model is based on the assumption of stupid learners
and superior experts. In my life, most of the ISD packages I've run into
were designed by people who are stupider than me. They're trying to
drag me down to the lowest common denominator."*

The world of the learner has changed dramatically. As predicted in *The Future of*

Work and, studied by Thomas Malone (2004), work has changed with the arrival of productivity software, digitalization of content, and connectedness through wireless devices or the Internet. To succeed, organizations have to compete globally, move fast, and be nimble and flexible. Thus, the learner is in constant flux. The job changes rapidly, learning time is short, and the learner must perform faster. She multi-tasks, telecommutes and relies on e-mail and teleconferencing to get more things done.

The demands for Rapid e-Learning reflect the increasing speed businesses need to get and stay ahead in the marketplace. This is confirmed in the responses to Question 14 in the e-Learning Guild study, which further shows that respondents feel that the great driving reason for rapid development is "short time-to-market

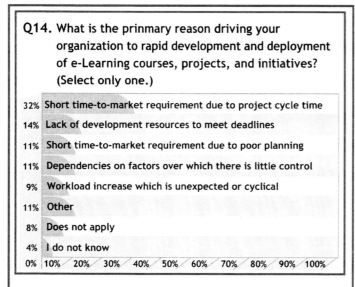

Q14. What is the prinmary reason driving your organization to rapid development and deployment of e-Learning courses, projects, and initiatives? (Select only one.)

32%	Short time-to-market requirement due to project cycle time
14%	Lack of development resources to meet deadlines
11%	Short time-to-market requirement due to poor planning
11%	Dependencies on factors over which there is little control
9%	Workload increase which is unexpected or cyclical
11%	Other
8%	Does not apply
4%	I do not know

0% 10% 20% 30% 40% 50% 60% 70% 80% 90% 100%

The most frequently cited driver for the use of rapid e-Learning methodology is shorter time-to-market. The need for development resources and poor planning on some past projects are also driving organizations to come up with ways to do rapid e-Learning. Apparently the hope and the promise here is to circumvent some of the barriers that have slowed down the development of e-Learning in the past. We were expecting poor planning and project management to be more of a factor, but it seems that this is not really much of an issue in most respondents' organizations.

requirements due to project cycle time." (See Figure 5-2, below).

Figure 5-2: Responses to Question 14

While we increase the speed for e-Learning development, we must address the learners' or users' needs to ensure we deliver a quality program.

To perform more efficiently in their jobs, e-learners are learning differently. The dynamic nature of the Internet, coupled with the fast pace of the workplace, have given birth to new learner behaviors. Today's e-learners:

- Need to access information quickly for immediate answers

- Want to apply solutions instantly

- Learn independently any time, anywhere they can

- Do not expect to retain or memorize information

- Jump around the material; no logic and sequence are necessary

- Use what they need at the moment

- Want quick entries and exits and to be able to pick up from where they have left off

I call these *e-Learning Behaviors,* and they are not compatible with traditional models of instructional design. (I coined the term "e-Learning Behaviors" to identify prevailing behaviors of learners while using the Internet and related technologies.) e-Learning Behaviors characterize people who are in 3-Minute e-Learning experiences. e-Learning Behaviors are the basis for the Organic e-Learning Design Principle: learners seek out "application points" or performance ideas.

We hamper our drive for rapid design and content development by not addressing this problem.

We need a new way of thinking, a new e-Learning Architecture so we can respond to the e-learners' needs while we increase the speed of the development process. When we establish the architecture, we will also discover ways to increase the speed and cut the costs of development.

This new way of thinking is what I call *"Organic e-Learning."* This is a process of designing e-Learning content that enables the learners to meet their personal needs. These needs are:

- The need to be in control of their learning

- The need to pursue what engages them at the moment

- The need to explore and discover

- The need to make learning a daily, personal, breathing and living experience

More About
e-Learning Architecture

Chapter 6

More About e-Learning Architecture

As we said, an e-Learning Architecture (e-LA) is a learning framework that meets the needs of e-learners and the demands of the business or organization.

The traditional Instructional Systems Design (ISD) is a learning framework that began as a response to the need to train massive numbers of people in the military. Over decades it became, and is today, the norm and standard for traditional training, conducted in classrooms, on the job, in seminars, and in lectures. ISD has philosophies, methodologies and processes.

Employing the ISD model in e-Learning and its development is not workable. ISD's linear, classroom-like, trainer-centered methods and production processes are not compatible with the inherent nature of e-Learning. e-Learning encourages high speed and a free flowing exchange of knowledge and information. It is unstructured and self-propelled – all of which are norms in the digital economy.

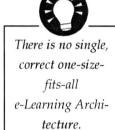

There is no single, correct one-size-fits-all e-Learning Architecture.

Organizational needs and differences in learners and their learning conditions make it impossible to develop a standard mold. However, whatever our e-Learning Architecture might be, it should meet these **new learning realities**:

- e-Learners have different needs due to the rapid demands of business conditions.

- e-Learners' expectations are fueled by the capabilities of information and communication technologies – in which speed, access, freedom and problem solving are the mode for doing things.

What is a good e-LA?

A well-defined e-LA helps dramatically in cutting costs and increasing the speed of development while it sustains quality results.

A building or a rocket has its own architecture to function properly. What is your e-LA?

The characteristics of a good e-LA

To summarize, a good e-LA:

- Focuses on meeting the organization's performance needs

- Identifies the quality outcomes suitable to e-learners

A building has an architecture

What is your e-Learning Architecture?

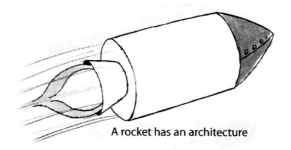

A rocket has an architecture

What is your e-Learning Architecture?

- Has components and purposes that are specific.

- Is easy to replicate and transfer from one person to another

- Is documented, shared and distributed

- Has software selected to fit a specific function

- Is easy to tweak and /or improve

- Is easy to determine and manage the costs

- Aids meeting timelines

- Has skill set requirements that are easy to determine and assess

Approaches to
e-Learning Architecture

Chapter  7

7

Approaches to e-Learning Architecture

There are essentially five general approaches to e-Learning Architecture (e-LA) that provide the foundations for many e-Learning programs. However, the effectiveness of each approach varies greatly. Let us examine our e-LA or lack of it, to see which model is closest to what we have:

- Basic Architecture: Talking head, book page-turning, lectures, PowerPoints

- Simulation, discovery, cases, scenario-based

- Virtual classroom, e.g. WebEx, Live Meeting, Breeze

- Online-help and references

- Performance Support Systems/Knowledge Management

> *e-Learning programs are only as good as the quality of thinking, planning and design of effective e-LA.*

Our task is to review the different approaches to determine how well they meet the characteristics of a good e-Learning Architecture.

How the different architectures relate

The chart on the next page illustrates some possible relationships of the different approaches. Our entry point or approach may vary depending on our needs. However, it is best that we construct an e-LA that matches our learners' needs and business requirements.

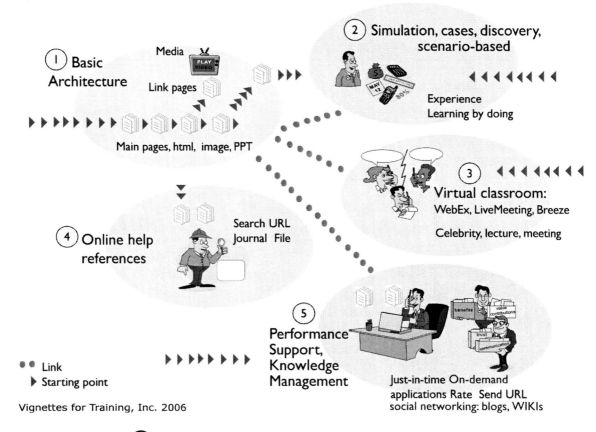

Figure 7-1: e-Learning Architecture: different approaches

Understanding the various e-LAs may help us choose an approach that best meets our rapid development and quality needs. Before looking at the basic e-LA, let us briefly consider the "default" approaches chosen by developers who have not understood the concept of effective e-LA.

Defaults that don't work: Talking heads, page turners, lectures, and PowerPoints

The "talking head" approach is a universal method in which one records a lecture or a presentation (usually as video) for delivery to learners. One often sees this in e-Learning programs because it is an easy transition from traditional training techniques to an e-Learning format. On the other hand, training manuals or PowerPoint files are often simply converted into e-Learning page-turners and slide shows. Unfortunately, there is no critical thinking applied to reorganizing, prioritizing or categorizing content to support the **e-Learning Behaviors** previously discussed.

Oh my gosh! Too many pages.

These methods are expedient, and there is plenty of software that converts them for online delivery as "e-Learning" (e.g. Breeze, Viewlet, Outstart, etc.). However, software may be effective or ineffective depending on the quality of the learning design. Unfortunately, much software merely converts training manuals and PowerPoints so they are viewable online. Many e-Learning programs are driven by the design of the software, not by needs of the e-learners.

Basic e-Learning Architecture - Organic, Lightweight and Effective

Chapter 8

Basic e-Learning Architecture - Organic, Lightweight and Effective

Chapter 8

Basic e-Learning Architecture - Organic, Lightweight and Effective

The Basic e-LA is the core and fundamental design of most e-Learning programs. It is easy to identify the basic design. We readily recognize them as page turners, slideshows, or talking heads. It is my estimate that roughly 95% of e-Learning programs currently published are basic designs. It is the most affordable, fastest and easiest way to publish e-Learning programs.

What is the significance of defining and establishing a clear Basic e-LA?

The goal of the basic 3-Minute Rapid e-Learning is to help learners to learn and apply knowledge to tasks to bring about results quickly. In other words, we want our target learners to learn in three minutes and perform on the job effectively. As we keep this in mind, we must take note of the reality that most of the significant stumbling blocks as well as greatest opportunities to Rapid e-Learning are found in the basic design. This is where learners spend most of their time. This is where the volume of development work is done. Furthermore, an effective Basic e-LA lays down the foundation of advanced architectures. Moreover, I suggest that poor implementation of a Basic e-LA leads to failed application of advanced architecture. In essence, we cannot build good programs on weak foundations.

Sometimes we think that it is easy to dismiss the basic design because it is, after all, composed of just pages, text and a few images. But this is worth pondering: why has Google been very successful even when it only presents text links? What makes text links appealing? When you do a search in Google, you initially get hundreds or thousands of links. Why do users accept, tolerate, or find valuable use for the links and text information?

What are root causes of ineffective basic designs?

Many of the problems that plague basic designs can be traced to the inability of developers and trainers to change their paradigms and mindsets from using

1.   *Boring page-turners into "kinda" entertaining and engaging lessons*

> *To make basic design more appealing, engaging and entertaining, there is a need to rethink how to organize, prioritize and present the content to the learners.*

Traditional training is about pushing and engaging the learner in order to motivate learning. The approach presupposes that to be effective the method has to be multimedia and interactive. Multimedia and interactivity have been thought of as key methods to increase attention and retention. However, in Chapter 4, we have learned that retaining knowledge is not a preferred e-Learning Behavior. And we have heard complaints that learners are not really patient with multimedia and interactivity when delivered online. Rather we have observed preferences for being able to have instant access to knowledge, quick entries and exits, and having the opportunity to quickly apply skills and knowledge to problem solving and performance issues.

Most organizations cannot afford to invest in multimedia and interactive designs, so they rely on the basic design as a main vehicle of their e-Learning programs. This brings us back to square one: without new thinking and improvements, the basic design becomes flat, boring, and uninteresting.

Instead of rethinking or redefining our expectations and approaches on how simple pages can serve the purpose of e-learners, we abandon this goal and push the use of multimedia slideshows and interactive exercises. We end up extending the basic pages and delivering them in slideshows and in narrated and animated interactivities without any change of approach. Of course, we know that when we simply repurpose the pages into a different media, the outcome is "kinda" entertaining and engaging, but sadly, still mostly half-baked. It is no wonder that most e-Learning developments are slow and costly, with little impact on performance.

To make basic design more appealing, engaging and entertaining, there is a need to rethink how to organize, prioritize and present the content to the learners.

2. *"Falling in love" with authoring software without critical thinking*

One of the biggest temptations in e-Learning development is embracing authoring software without first going through an instructional design of the content. For many of us who have taken this route, we discover quickly that the software is only as good as the amount of creative thinking and instructional thought applied to the lessons.

Basic pages have great value in e-Learning delivery. However, it is easier and more convenient to jump and start pounding the keyboard or downloading a software package to migrate or repurpose the pages into an e-Learning format. A good example is the knee-jerk reaction of simply using PowerPoint presentations as e-Learning lessons without doing anything different with the PowerPoint presentations. Katherine Horton delivered a presentation in www.eLearningGuild.com online workshops entitled *"PowerPoint: The Basis for Everything!"* In this session she provided ideas on how to design Power Points for e-Learning delivery. It is worth checking out her presentation.

Beyond PowerPoint, we encounter the same problems in using authoring tools, such as Lectora, Viewlet, Captivate and Flash, and many others. We are told by vendors that we can develop our lessons over the weekend. In most cases this is true. But what they fail to inform us is that this is a technical action and not an instructional design or creative action.

There is a need to clearly understand that, before applying a software solution, there are three outcomes that need to occur:

a. An instructional thought process;
b. A documentation on how to communicate the instructional thought;
c. A plan with costing and timelines based on the instructional thought.

It is only with the above information that everyone has a clear idea about what and how to transform the content for e-Learning.

The purpose of Appendix B is to provide a step-by-step guide for arriving at these three outcomes.

For many of us who have taken this route, we discover quickly that the software is only as good as the amount of creative thinking and instructional thought applied to the lessons.

3. *Mechanical and technical content devoid of life*

Another significant root cause of the flaws in basic design, also in most interactive design, is the dependence on technical and factual content as the basis for the e-Learning lessons.

Training content is usually written by SMEs (Subject Matter Experts) who are technicians, engineers or experts on a subject. They are not trainers, instructional designers or developers. We need SMEs in the e-Learning process. However, the tendency to rely wholly on input of the SMEs leads to ineffective e-Learning programs.

Learners learn best when they learn with *emotional* or contextual content side by side with the technical content. Emotional content is *Organics* consisting of stories, anecdotes, examples, illustrations, cases, stories and other related methods. Organic content provides the context and adds the meaning to the technical content. For example, a learner learns easily the function of software if the function is related to a real-life situation, case or application. I coined the term "**e-Learning Organics®**" to signify applying *Organics* in e-Learning design as opposed to using mechanics or mechanical content.

In classroom training, organic content is usually presented by the trainer. A good trainer uses real-life experiences to make the technical content more meaningful and, therefore, useful to the learners. Unfortunately, in the process of converting training content to e-Learning, the technical information is transferred while the organic content is omitted. That is why most e-Learning programs that only present technical content are difficult to learn and require so much effort to understand.

Earlier I stated that the same problem occurs in interactive design. If trainers and developers do not use *Organics* in basic design, they will likely not use organics in highly interactive designs like games, exercises, and simulations. Learning to design e-Learning with the use of *Organics* is a must step in basic design and even more so in advanced interactive designs.

Laying down a good foundation for the Basic e-LA will help cut costs, increase the speed of production and make 3-Minute e-Learning programs effective. This is where we gain at least 70% reduction in costs and time.

See more details and the step-by-step implementation of "Organic e-Learning Design Process" in Appendix B.

Key Ideas - Basic e-Learning Architecture

We should note that we can transform page-turners and slide shows effectively, in other words making sure they are organized to support *e-Learning Behaviors*. The content must be categorized, organized, written and displayed in order to:

- Present must-learn and performance-focused content in main pages or immediately apparent pages.

- Make principles, objectives and key ideas immediately visible where they "must be seen."

- Make references, guides, tools, and resources secondary links.

- Keep the number of pages ("screens") per lesson short (3 to 5 pages – never 10, 20 or more pages).

- Present a small amount of text per page (50 words).

- Use an image to reinforce the message in the content of a page.

- End each short lesson of 3 to 5 pages with a short review (not a test for assessing retention, but a review to help learners apply the ideas).

- Eliminate scrolling.

- Use *Organics* -- stories, cases, illustrations, real-life examples, anecdotes, and metaphors as a writing approach; avoid lecture or telling tone.

- Limit slide shows to no more than one minute; allow e-learners to move in and out, forward and backward, and to stop easily.

- Maintain a conversational mode while guiding (instructing) e-learners.

- Allow e-learners to move randomly anywhere they want to go, any time.

Organic e-Learning design has its roots in e-Learning Behaviors - where the design encourages freedom of choice. It promotes a natural, living and breathing learning experience. This is opposed to the rigid and controlled-by- trainer learning experience.

How to Make the Basic Architecture Work for Rapid Development?

Chapter

How to Make the Basic Architecture Work for Rapid Development

Reducing the amount of content to focus on "application points", "must learns" and performance-result areas will increase the speed of development, reduce the cost, and meet e-Learners' needs. "Must learns" are focused on knowledge or skills that are critical in performing tasks.

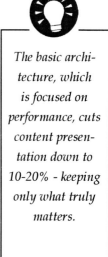

The basic architecture, which is focused on performance, cuts content presentation down to 10-20% - keeping only what truly matters.

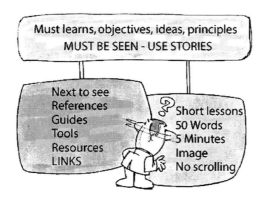

Figure 9-1: The Basic Architecture is this simple

Here are three very specific benefits of developing using the basic architecture:

Basic architecture is lightweight and focused on content

In most programs we would probably find around 10-20% "must learns" and "performance outcomes, key principles, objectives and ideas." The rest would be references, resources, procedures, policies – which make up 90% of a program. "Must learns" are part of the content critical to the application to a task or performance. Focusing on presenting "must learns" and "principles and key ideas" allows us to focus time and effort on this 10% of the content, rather than the 90% that is secondary in value. When it is time to present the bulk of the information, it is best put into HTMLs, PDFs, Word documents, etc. Of course, we can expect the subject matter experts (SMEs) will object. For them **everything** — all content — is important.

Basic architecture enables the e-learner

e-Learners can move around, go in and out quickly and randomly, select what they need and focus on "must learn" content for immediate use. Their ability to move around randomly becomes possible only because we lay out the content for them in easy ways, i.e. short lessons, short pages, less reading, use of images to convey messages, no scrolling, etc. **This design cuts down by 75% the burden** on
e-Learners of being required to follow a sequence and being forced to turn every page.

Basic architecture helps in gathering and organizing content from SMEs more efficiently

The e-Learning Guild "Rapid e-Learning Development Research Report" tells us that many of the designers who responded to the survey point to working with SMEs as an area where Rapid e-Learning could provide an innovative solution. Sixty five percent of the respondents admit that "SMEs give us content in any manner, and we work with it." Broken down, 70% of the designers use interviews and 42% use a standardized template to gather information. (See Figures 9-1 and 9-2.)

Joe Pulichino, the e-Learning Guild's Director of Research, states:

"Clearly, this is an area where we can have a classic trade-off between speed and quality. It is possible that some of the greatest innovations in Rapid e-Learning practice will come in the area of getting content from SMEs faster without compromising the quality of the content."

Q18. Which one of the following statements is most often true concerning how Subject Matter Experts (SMEs) in your organization provide content to instructional designers and developers? (Select one.)

65%	SMEs give us content in any manner and we work with it
14%	SMEs fill out specific design forms which we work with
7%	SMEs input content directly using development tools
3%	SMEs do not provide us with content
6%	Other
3%	Does not apply
2%	I do not know

0% 10% 20% 30% 40% 50% 60% 70% 80% 90% 100%

The majority of respondents indicated they work with the content in whatever way they receive it from the SME. Would having templates that the SME's populate with content shorten the development cycle? On the other hand, would it take the SME's longer to get the content to the designers if they had to use templates? Perhaps it is a mixture of both.

 Figure 9-1: Responses to Question 18

Q19. What tools do you employ with Subject Matter Experts (SMEs) to help you develop e-Learning content? (Select all that apply.)

70%	Interviews
42%	Standardized Word or Excel templates to gather information
30%	Email questionaires or surveys
25%	Specific content structured questionaires
22%	Focus groups
11%	Other
7%	Does not apply

0% 10% 20% 30% 40% 50% 60% 70% 80% 90% 100%

An interview process (70%) is the most common method for engaging SMEs to help in the content development process. Questionnaires using standardized templates (42%) is a much less frequently used method. In some respects this is one of the more labor intensive and important areas in the development cycle, because if the content is flawed the final product is likely to have little value. Clearly, this is an area where we can have a classic trade-off between speed and quality. It is possible that some of the greatest innovations in rapid e-Learning practice will come in the area of getting content from SMEs faster without compromising the quality of the content.

 Figure 9-2: Responses to Question 19

In many of the projects I have been involved with, working with the SMEs has often been a major cause for delays, high costs and poor quality. As in traditional training, we place them on a pedestal -- the "celebrity" and "super-trainer" lecturer in an expert role. In many situations SMEs are overrated and irrelevant. They are busy. Their instructional model is most often the lecture. And they insist on presenting linear information. Their focus is on their expertise rather than the
e-learners' needs.

In advanced e-Learning models, which are organic and dynamic support systems, SMEs continue to be important, but their role supports the process rather than being the center of the universe (which we will discuss in later sections).

Moreover, if we must work effectively with SMEs, we need a sound e-Learning Architecture; otherwise, we will continue to succumb to the whims, style and instructional model of our SMEs. They will take the most familiar and habitual path.

An e-Learning Architecture will provide several benefits when managing SMEs. Specifically, we (the designers) will be able to:

- Educate SMEs on an e-Learning Architecture based on what works for our e-learners. (Without an alternative, they lecture us to death.)

- Assist SMEs to organize, categorize, write and display the content that meets the standard of our architecture (structuring their contribution so it is easy and time-efficient for them).

Ensure that our content has been tested and is proven and consistent because it follows our architecture design (to avoid changing our design depending on

How to Transform Our e-Learning Architecture

Chapter 10

How to Transform Our e-Learning Architecture

The resources that follow can help us transform our e-Learning Architecture (e-LA) through a specific procedure and process. These guides will allow us to better manage working with SMEs in order to speed up the process, cut cost, and deliver quality programs. For more details, please see Appendix B.

There are a total of four guides:

- Writing modules, lessons, and pages

- Guide for interviewing SMEs

- How to develop images

- Content developer and writer checklist

Writing modules, lessons, and pages: A guide

> Writing lessons and pages requires both a good understanding of the content and creative skills in telling stories. It also requires an instructional knowledge of how to position content based on its hierarchy of value to the learning process.

The purpose of writing lessons and pages

Text is the means by which most, if not all, content is delivered for participants to learn the subject. Writing supports the learning process by communicating:

- Relevant topics to the audience

- Specific skill or knowledge to be learned

- Engaging stories, cases, metaphors, illustrations and examples, as well as other methods

What makes up the required preparation for writing?

Research and study content thoroughly. Categorize content into four groups:

- Application points, performance outcomes, goals, principles, key ideas

- Processes, tasks, steps, procedures

- Tools, references, forms

- People, relationships, coordination

Identify the must-learn items from the key ideas or content; differentiate them from "nice to know" or optional content. Organize the content into modules, lessons, and pages.

Write out a detailed outline of what goes into each lesson and corresponding pages; reduce the lessons and pages into vignettes or small segments that contain key ideas and priority knowledge to be imparted.

Prepare the organics: the stories, case studies, metaphors, etc. that go with the lesson. Create ideas that will be converted into images (see the guide to creating images in the following sections). Select and arrange the general ideas for the links, downloads, references, etc.

Note that preparing the above materials, even as an outline or a top-level view, aids greatly in writing. Without this preparation, writing will take longer and will be more difficult.

Structure of Modules, Lessons and Pages

Modules consist of lessons, and lessons consist of pages.

A good practice is to make short lessons that allow learners to review smaller amounts of information. They also require only a few minutes of study. Ideally, a lesson consists of a small content set that participants can learn in a few minutes. By a "few minutes" we mean 3 minutes, more or less, depending the participants. Lessons allow quick entry and exit, or quick access to details provided in links.

Lessons should have 5 to 7 main pages, and the last main page is a review, a test or an exercise. If there are more than 7 main pages in a lesson, try to divide the lesson into smaller ones. Having more than 7 pages means that there are too many details in the main pages – the details may be more appropriately converted to links.

Limit each main page to 50 words. Main pages contain performance outcomes, goals, key ideas, principles or must-learn ideas. For example:

- Page 1: Introduction, gain attention
- Page 2: Performance outcomes, goals, key ideas ("application points")
- Page 3: Key principles
- Page 4: Introduce a detailed idea
- Page 5: Review page

Jump pages are link pages that summarize or introduce links that are external references or that are large bodies of text or content. The jump page provides synthesis or key highlights that the reader ought to learn or study in the linked body of text or details.

Link pages are pages containing detailed information or in-depth lessons on processes, tasks, steps, procedures, tools, references, forms, people or relationships. We can use many methods for creating link pages including:

- Download
- PowerPoint files or slide shows
- MS Word documents
- MS Excel spreadsheets
- Video
- Audio
- Interactive Flash

- Games

- Case studies

- Charts and forms

- PDF manuals

- Assignments

- OJT

Learners drill down to the content in link pages. Link pages must be easy to enter, navigate, and exit. Lessons presented in link pages are interactive and more engaging.

Introduce to learners in the main pages the contents of the jump or link pages. These introductions must be compelling and benefits-driven to entice and encourage participants to click the links.

Each lesson ends with a review page. Review pages have many uses. A review page is for reflection, checklists and directionals (guides or instructions). A review page in the middle of a lesson can help participants reflect or interact with the content, coach or peers. An important function of review pages is to provide a counter-check or feedback to participants on their progress in this lesson and link pages. Review pages also contain the programming codes needed to enable tracking. Reviews must redirect participants to content as needed for study. Differentiate assessment tests from review questions. Do not confuse these two types of questions. Separate assessment tests by putting them at the end of the module of program, for example, a test for certification.

Practical tips in assembling the lesson pages and writing

Start by writing detailed outlines for each module, lesson and main page.

Remember: "More organics than mechanics." Mechanics are factual statements or descriptions of the content. Mechanics are static. Organics are stories, real life examples, that add meaning and context to the content. People learn best through stories and real illustrations. Use organics to introduce content. Write text and prepare graphics and other elements to highlight the organics.

Facilitating cues (keeping a conversation) and guides are essential. Use directionals and interface design to facilitate, guide, coach and prod learners to study the content. Directionals are statements that tell the learner to do something or ask a question that requires an answer. "Click the link," "Study the example," "Reflect on this for a moment," "What would you do?"

Write from a first-person view to make it friendly. Set a conversational tone, not too formal. State learning objectives and outcomes as benefit statements rather than the usual "you will learn..." or "the objectives are..." Use active words, vivid examples and illustrations.

Examples

Please see the writing and assembly pages in as referred to in **Appendix B** and provided in the web site **www.vignettestraining.com**.

Guide for interviewing SMEs

This interview guide follows the Organic e-Learning Design Process that helps SMEs and instructional designers work together to organize content for 3-Minute e-Learning and Rapid e-Learning.

For more details, please the SME Interview Guide in Appendix C.

The focus of 3-Minute Rapid e-Learning is rapid development and delivery, as well as organization of content that allows learners to control the way they learn.

It is responsive to immediate problem-solving or performance of tasks.

It is important, before asking the series of interview questions, to discuss with the SME the need for 3- Minute Rapid e-Learning methodology. Win over the SME on the benefits of Rapid e-Learning.

Interview questions:

1. What is the topic of the content?

2. Describe the scope by breaking down the content into major key groups — as an outline, a flow chart, or as components or sub-parts.

3. Who are the audience or users of the content? Describe their characteristics.

4. Describe the performance outcomes required from the job or function of the users or audience.

5. Of all these performance outcomes, which ones have the most immediate impact on performance, costs, speed, savings and pay-offs? Prioritize these outcome areas in terms of their impact.

6. What conditions, circumstances, or forces in actual situations make the top outcome areas more important than the others? For example:

   - What is important for the business, the organization or the learner?

   - If the nature of the job is such that there is a high turnover, and you may only have the person on the job for one to four weeks, what will be the performance outcomes?

   - If the function is highly specialized (e.g. that of doctors) what would be the most important performance areas?

   - The conditions and demands of the job for performance dictate the priority of learning or training. In your case and topic content, what would be the circumstances and what are the priority outcomes?

7. Now that we have identified the most critical or "top of the list" performance outcomes and the conditions that required the outcomes, what part of the content answers these concerns?

    • Let's follow the 80/20 rule where 20% of the content might make greater contributions than the other 80%. What are the 20% critical few content items that match the priority performance outcomes? (Applications points.)

8. In each of the content items selected, or performance content, categorize the type of content as:

    • Performance outcomes, application points, key ideas, principles and critical must-learn points – central themes and knowledge that are key for learners to understand. (Can't miss these!)

    • References, tools and guides – for example, documents, tips, and information resources.

    • Processes, policies, and methods – the ways, steps, and how-to's of the tasks.

    • Relationships and coordination with people. (These are the key people with whom to coordinate and relate, or to whom to report while performing the tasks.)

By now we are analyzing the content as granular pieces in order to decide what is valuable content and information. Most often, content will have this distribution:

    • Performance outcomes, key ideas, principles – 10 to 20% of the content

    • References, processes, relationship and coordination – 80%

It is important for the SME to understand that not all content is a "must" when looking at performance areas. Only a few key content items matter at any one time, as dictated by the performance outcomes.

9. To deliver the content effectively, relate a story, metaphor, real life example, case or illustration that makes the 20% critical content *come alive to the participants*. These are the ***e-Learning Organics***.

    Learners will understand the content best if they experience it with a story or the "organics."

    Ask the SME to dramatize the story.

    • What can go wrong, or what has gone wrong, in failing to apply the performance areas and content?

    • What will be greatest benefit, or what can really go right?

    Obtaining these "organics" helps to make the e-Learning experience more "human" and "real-life" for the participant.

10. What exercise, activity, on-the-job assignments, real-life tasks, or software and tools can we ask the learner to perform or use that will help apply the critical performance content? We call these the "applications." (The applications are important to help us design interactive experiences to allow better training or immediate application of the performance outcomes.)

11. After generating the above information, can we organize it into short, concise and focused modules, lessons, and pages with a focus on performance outcome content and critical must-have content?

    Structurally divide the content into modules and lessons based on the information provided. We now have a meaningful organization of content that aids in rapid development while keeping high quality and value.

Some additional guidelines:

- Start e-Learning lessons with organics and relate everything to them.
- Focus on presenting "must learns" that meet performance outcomes.
- Make references, tools and relationship types secondary links or information that learners may opt to study but which are not required.
- Make lessons short, concise, to the point.
- Apply interactivities only with organics; without organics, interactivities are ineffective.

How to develop images

Selecting and designing images requires a thoughtful process. Images communicate and reinforce the content to be imparted. Images create a more lasting impression or a more complete presentation of the content and, thus, contribute to better learning.

How do we pick the right image?

- Pick the image that shows the concept, fact, and/or emotions of the content.
- Pick or select the image that tells a story or theme that transfers the meaning of the content.

What makes a good image?

- Action oriented – shows action, ideas and people
- Appeals to emotions – appeals to the emotional side of participants
- Elicits a reaction – speaks to and gets the attention of participants
- Instant message – shows instantly the idea of the page or the content

- Familiarity – shows familiar themes and a creative look

- Exaggerated – calls attention quickly; extreme negative or positive

- Aesthetically pleasing – high production values and creative work added, not just common clip art

- Image with expressions, gestures, emotions (not stale or static images)

- Culturally or socially acceptable to the participant

Practical tips on production

Producing a good image is a costly and time-consuming process. There are ways to reduce these factors.

- Combine several images to build one image that communicates the message.
- Use cartoons or illustrations as images when the idea is difficult to capture in a photo.
- Sometimes using large text on key points on the graphic does the job.
- Stay consistent with styles, fonts, colors, characters.
- Reuse images on different pages to reinforce ideas. However, when reusing, make a change in the image, such as cropping, zooming or lifting part of the image.
- Treat images with visual effects, such as backgrounds, shades, filters and other creative touches in order to add quality.
- Keep images clean and neat, allowing the message to dominate, rather than the style.
- Ideas come first – the style helps convey the ideas.

I have placed some examples of the above interactivities online at **www.vignettestraining.com.**

Content developer and writer checklist

It is wise to go through the following checklist and find out how many we can answer with a resounding "YES!" before finalizing our content for submission and integration into the Learning Management System (LMS).

Content – Style

❐ Are the facts on the page presented with a human-interest angle (organics)?

- Is there a story, anecdote, illustration or case study being told in the page?

- Will the story appeal to the target audience?

- Is the page fun to read, friendly and easily accessible (understandable) to learners?

❐ Is there a smooth transition from one page to the next?

- Is the page coherent with the overall theme and/or story?

- Is there a logical flow of topics from page to page?

- Is this page consistent with the previous pages written?

❐ Are the key words and ideas in bold face?

- Will looking only at the bold words give the learner the gist of the page?

- Are the bold words really the key ideas of the page?

- Are some ideas in bullet points? (only applies to some pages)

- Are the ideas presented with bullet points best presented in this way?

- Are there no more than three pages in a lesson using bullet points?

Structure – Technical requirements

❑   Is the page written with correct grammar, structure and spelling?

❑   Does the page follow the correct structure?

- Is the correct worksheet format being used?

- Does the lesson page have 50 words or fewer?

- Does the lesson have six pages or fewer?

- Is there a one-page lesson review for this lesson?

- Is the page correctly labeled?

❑   Did we avoid putting too much information on one page?

- Does the page cover one main idea/key goal/principle?

- Does the page have only one main idea?

- For those pages that are better explained with links to reference materials (only applies to some):

    o Have forms, charts, policies and long documents that need to be used as reference materials been linked to link pages?

    o Are the reference materials in PDF format (ideally)?

    o Is the summary/overview of the reference material in the main lesson page?

    o Was a link page used for long references? (By contrast, a jump page has a summary or instruction to readers showing what to look for in the main body content they are linking to.)

❏ Are there facilitative cues and/or instructions on the page?

- Are the instructions informative?

- Do the instructions give the learner an idea of the link contents?

- Are the learners provided with learning cues, benefits, tips or very brief descriptions that describe the links or buttons before they click any link or button? (For example: "Click here to see the ten most valuable solutions.")

Images

❏ Does the image reflect the emotional experience of the page?

❏ Will the image capture the learner's attention?

- Is the image a little exaggerated? (Exaggerated images gain more attention, which is what we want.)

- Is the image humorous, when appropriate?

- Is the image provocative or engaging in some way?

❏ Does the image have an appropriate caption? (Key word captions make it easy for learners to see the key ideas of the page.)

- Is the caption short?

- Is the caption catchy?

- Is the caption in line with the page content?

Writing reviews and evaluations

☐ Is there a review at the end of each lesson so the participant can reflect on the key points? Reviews are either check questions, reflective questions or checklists. It is not necessary to use test questions all the time.

- Is the review page of questions really short, containing only three to five questions?

- Are the questions focused on the key points of the lesson?

- The lesson review should complement the type of content discussed in the lesson.
  - o For a lesson involving a process, was the sequence type review used?

  - o For a lesson discussion on a number of products or services, was a matching type review used?

  - o For a lesson better understood by anecdotes or stories, was the essay-type review used?

- Was a choice made to present a fill-in-the-blank, single-choice or multiple-choice type of review instead of true/false?

- The review length (number of questions) depends on the type of review given.
  - o If it is a true/false or multiple-choice test, is there a minimum of three questions?

  - o If it is a sequence or matching type of review, is there only one question asked so as not to overwhelm the participant?

  - o If it is an essay review, are the questions limited to a maximum of three, especially if the questions require a long answer?

- Do the choices in the questions not give away the answers?

- For lesson reviews, is there a reference page that participants can refer to in case they do not get the correct answer?

- Is there a review at the end of the module to discuss its key points?

- Would a module review be more engaging by using of Flash or other software interactive software?

- Does the module review have an evaluation with these points asked:

  o How were the learners' experiences?

  o What are their suggestions (content and/or technical)?

  o Does the program include pre- and post-tests to gauge the learners' knowledge before and after taking the program?

  o Is the pre-test composed of 10 to 20 questions?

  o Is there a program evaluation, asking for user feedback of the program as a whole?

Other resources - also in Appendix B and C

Web site references.

Please visit the web site **www.vignettestraining.com** to access examples and illustrations for each chapter.

Software and Tools Serve the Purpose of e-Learning Architecture, Not the Other Way Around

Chapter 11

Software and Tools Serve the Purpose of e-Learning Architecture, Not the Other Way Around

In the eLearning Guild Study cited earlier, respondents have reported that they see "Rapid development tools" as one of the characteristics of "Rapid e-Learning Development." (See Figure 11-1). The study suggests that although tools are important, it is also important to shorten the design process.

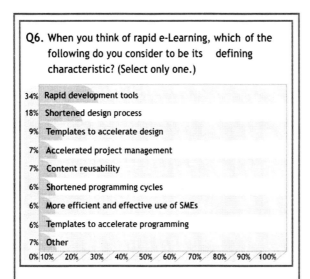

Q6. When you think of rapid e-Learning, which of the following do you consider to be its defining characteristic? (Select only one.)

34%	Rapid development tools
18%	Shortened design process
9%	Templates to accelerate design
7%	Accelerated project management
7%	Content reusability
6%	Shortened programming cycles
6%	More efficient and effective use of SMEs
6%	Templates to accelerate programming
7%	Other

0% 10% 20% 30% 40% 50% 60% 70% 80% 90% 100%

We asked survey respondents to select only one choice because we wanted to see what the single most common defining characteristic of rapid e-Learning development was. According to survey respondents, "Rapid development tools" (34%) trump "Shortened design process" (18%) by a nearly 2-to-1 margin. It is intereting to see that this characteristic is most frequently associated with rapid e-Learning development, especially when compared to the results of the next question where "Content review and approval" and "Access to subject matter experts" are cited as the two factors that most frequently slow down the development of e-Learning products. in this case the "More efficient and effective use of SME's" might have received a lower score because other choices were deemed to be more significant and only one choice was permitted for this question. Shotening the design process, the use of templates and content reusability are ways to shorten the development cycle, and when you group all three together they make up a significant 31%. Therefore, while many respondents view rapid e-Learning through the tools that are used, just as many see the importance of process as a factor in setting the speed of the development.

 Figure 11-1: Responses to Question 6

Often, the wrong fit between the e-Learning Architecture (e-LA) and the software features and capabilities causes delays and costs in e-Learning development. A fuzzy definition of an e-LA usually leads to these problems:

- Wasting time looking for the right software feature without the guide of an e-Learning Architecture. This is like trying to find a needle in a haystack when the e-Learning Architecture could serve as metal detector.

- Allowing IT or software producers to decide which software meets our needs without prescribing an e-Learning Architecture.

- Purchasing software that is either too weak to get desired results, or too powerful so it takes too long to learn to use, or too costly to purchase.

Having a clearly defined architecture allows us to achieve the right balance between easy, fast, and inexpensive software and advanced software.

Having a clearly defined architecture allows us to achieve the right balance between easy, fast and inexpensive software, and advanced software. It allows us to select the right people with the appropriate skill sets. We can also maximize the full capability of the software when we know the end results we wish to derive.

There are many decisions to be made in selecting the right software, but paramount is using our e-Learning Architecture to achieve both the quality program and the right software. The e-LA simplifies our software selection. For Rapid e-Learning development, we must focus on the quality outcome, use the minimal capabilities of the software and minimize being distracted by software functions and capabilities that are not supporting our architecture.

For example, it is acceptable to use PowerPoint or HTML for basic page designs. However, merely importing classroom presentations into an e-Learning vehicle without reorganizing the content to meet e-learners' needs can have a disastrous effect.

Please see Appendix B for discussions on matching design with software and tools.

Look for the right fit

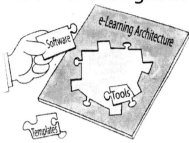

Checklist for software decisions

☐ Does it support our e-LA?

☐ What are the key strengths and weaknesses of the software?

☐ How easy is it to learn and implement?

☐ What is the learning curve required? Does it match our available people?

☐ What part of the architecture does the software support best?

☐ What type of integration is required with all other software being used in our project?

☐ In many instances, an e-Learning program requires more than one type of software. How effectively are we combining the software to have a seamless learning experience?

☐ Based on our long and short term needs and design, how can we justify and compute the returns for purchasing this software?

☐ How flexible is the software? What happens if we need to convert our content into another format or software? Can we move our content? Do we have freedom to control our core assets?

❏ Does the software allow us to maintain a consistent, aesthetic and high-quality style?

❏ What is the genesis or origin of the software? Is it a desktop or web-enabled tool?

❏ How responsive and effective is the software support?

❏ What are the licensing or acquisition costs and ongoing maintenance costs?

❏ Is the software being pushed by someone from our team because it reflects his or her skill set? Is the IT group pushing the software with or without our design consideration?

Software "religions"

Avoid the quagmire of software "religions." Software producers, developers and vendors have very strong convictions about their software. This is natural, the same way some people are hooked on the belief that ISD applies very well to e-Learning.

Understand that these beliefs stem from the nature of their jobs, the technology standards and processes.

So, when we are in a situation where we have to confront software decisions, let us go back to our e-LA as the basis for the decisions (this is important to meet e-Learner needs) and test the software decisions based on common sense business standards: costs, savings, efficiencies, reliability, function, and performance.

Let us seek out a software or IT champion that has some "business sense."

Set the design for
software to follow

Software
developer
producer

e-Learning
designer

An Interactive Format Uses Simulation, Discovery, Cases or a Scenario-Based Approach

Chapter 12

An Interactive Format Uses Simulation, Discovery, Cases or a Scenario-Based Approach

Sometimes, learners need to experience and discover answers for themselves. In these situations, learners will benefit from an interactive method. Usually, these methods are best for complex learning requirements where the need for interactivity with the content is high. The interactive method is valuable for e-learners. However, the production is usually expensive and slow. It does not have to be. Many interactive designs are bloated with content. So instead of producing all the content as interactive forms that require scripts and complex coding, the interactivity should be focused on what matters most.

Interactivity helps learners "experience," reflect on or review the subject matter or content. It engages learners, allowing them to explore and discover the answers or ideas for themselves, rather than merely telling or lecturing to them.

Criteria for selecting interactivity for Rapid e-Learning

Not all subjects qualify for interactive treatment (see Figure 12-1). There are several criteria for identifying content best addressed in an interactive format. Some content may require emotional experience and personal reflection or human interaction; or it may require participants to practice, drill or act on something to ensure they understand and acquire a skill. This would include skill and knowledge that are:

Online interactivity enhances learning in a less risky environment. It allows trainees to have several tries without the usual time pressures of on-the-job training. Online interactive experiences reduce the time and costs of learning, usually costing less than face-to-face instruction does.

- **Essential to performance** ("application points") – This content is necessary to learn in order to perform a task. This content represents the key essential skills or knowledge required by the learner .

- **Difficult to learn** – We want to ensure that learners have more time learning difficult aspects of our content. Some skills or knowledge deficiencies may cause frequent errors on the job or lead to more confusion.

- **Causes of errors and waste** – This is content that is typically a source for errors or mistakes that lead to high costs and waste.

- **"Hands-on"** – This content must be experienced, such as learning how to calibrate equipment or giving and receiving feedback.

Why is it important to rapid development that we be selective about what content will become interactivity?

Not all content should be in interactive form. Don't put into interactive format content that can be delivered in plain text, images and references. If we can determine that only 10% of our content really needs to be interactive, we will drastically reduce the time required for development. Appropriate use of interactivity also helps learners focus on what is truly important and what matters – which is one of their needs.

Here are some examples:

- In a negotiation program, listening is a difficult skill to acquire. Develop an interactivity focusing on listening skills.

- In teaching the use of a complex business form, create interactivity about the most complex and misunderstood part of the form, rather than about all the parts of the form.

- In software training, pick the areas that learners must not forget. Develop interactive exercises around that content. Do not provide interactivity for showing simple tasks, such as logging in or where to get support. This content is better explained in a graphic or text.

- Avoid using interactivity that is not really needed just to allow learners to click something, providing activity for its own sake. Presenting interactivity in slide show formats or linear flow presentations (simply clicking the "Next" button after reading the slide) is a waste of time and money. We can present the slide show in text or in HTML without adding interactive Flash.

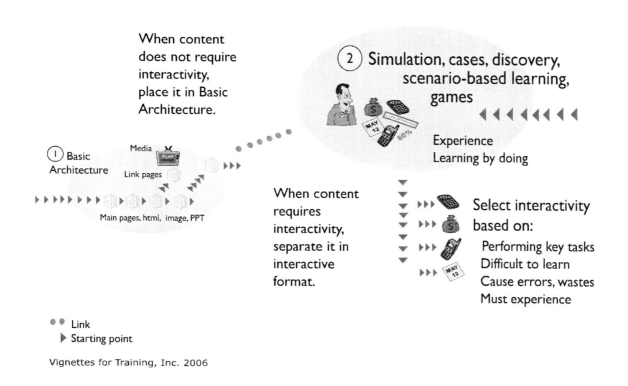

e-Learning Architecture: Different Approaches

When content does not require interactivity, place it in Basic Architecture.

② Simulation, cases, discovery, scenario-based learning, games ◀◀◀◀◀◀◀

Experience
Learning by doing

① Basic Architecture

Media

Link pages

Main pages, html, image, PPT

When content requires interactivity, separate it in interactive format.

Select interactivity based on:

Performing key tasks
Difficult to learn
Cause errors, wastes
Must experience

Link
▶ Starting point

Vignettes for Training, Inc. 2006

 Figure 12-1: Simulation, cases, discovery, scenario-based approach

Interactive e-Learning designs

This is good advice: Be a collector! Develop and accumulate a variety of interactive e-Learning designs. After testing designs for effectiveness, as well as for cost of production and speed of delivery, we can organize them so our team members can readily access them as templates or models. To make our interactive design effective, let us skillfully use the discovery process: immerse, touch, feel, handle, manipulate.

There are different types of interactivity, but all are primarily self-paced, and e-Learners interact with the content online. For example:

- **Knowledge Mapping** – Helps learners to understand the content because information is organized effectively and flows properly. The result allows learners to retain overall perspective while learning the content.

- **Route Interaction or Learning** – Consists of exercises that help learners remember and recall specific information.

- **Technical Simulation** – Enables the learner to virtually touch, feel and experience the material that needs to be learned. It also helps to explain complex information.

- **Conceptual and Judgment** – Used for helping learners understand and apply concepts that call for judgment and decision-making.

- **Emotional and Behavioral Simulation** – Learners confront or experience the issues from which they need to learn. Simulation and scenario-based exercises are good examples.

Visit the e-Learning Architect Basic and Advance Flash Galleries to preview examples of the above interactivities.

Please visit the web site **www.vignettestraining.com** to view more examples of the different types of interactivities.

Virtual Classroom (VC), e.g. WebEx, LiveMeeting, Breeze, etc.

Chapter 13

Virtual Classroom (VC), e.g. WebEx, LiveMeeting, Breeze, etc.

Virtual classrooms (VCs), e.g. WebEx, LiveMeeting, Breeze, Elluminate, etc. are extensions of the classroom or face-to-face setting where featured speakers or lecturers present their ideas. Another key function of VCs is to be able to share applications. The trainer or technical support person can see how the trainee is performing functions on his or her PC. VCs are also good tools for collaboration support and meetings. Most VCs record the sessions so that participants can replay them. VCs also provide registration and tracking services.

Where do virtual classrooms fit into an e-Learning Architecture?

Virtual classrooms are good tools for rapid deployment and presentation. All we need is a presentation (often a PowerPoint file), an account with a provider, and a scheduled session time and - Voila! - we have a training session. This is the VC's greatest asset – simple and immediate availability. However, just using VCs to support our e-Learning program does not meet most of the e-learners' needs. Usually, the presentation is a lecture. Even worse, it's a lecture where the lecturer does not know if the audience is paying attention!

VCs work superbly, according to Bersin & Associates, if the lecturer is a celebrity or a folk hero that the audience loves or follows. The value for the learner, in this case, is to be inspired by a charismatic presenter. This is well and good, and probably the best use of VCs.

Criteria for deploying virtual classrooms

To help participants apply ideas from VC presentations, provide links to a basic e-Learning Architecture and recorded lessons. Allow participants more time to interact with the content.

The Celebrity Factor or application sharing

107

Virtual classrooms as stand-alone e-Learning programs usually will not accomplish all of the results we want with our learners. However, the VC's biggest values is in one-to-group meetings, small group meetings, collaboration and application sharing. We should maximize VCs for the right reasons and avoid making them our only e-Learning program.

Since VCs are synchronous sessions (participants have to be on the same schedule), we use them to provide quick response to learner needs or to provide high-value interaction or presentations. Both cases assume that only the expert can provide the information. The event can then be presented as a session with the experts or a leader. It is best to avoid using VCs for basic presentations, such as lectures. Learners can be easily e-mailed or provided a link to the basic information.

Provide basic knowledge either by using the reference online learning approach discussed below, or by using a basic structure e-Learning design. This allows learners to review basic information prior to the scheduled VC session.

When providing the handouts and references, make them searchable text. This allows learners the ability to review the link and search for the right information faster.

To help participants apply ideas from the VC presentations, provide links to a basic e-Learning Architecture. Allow them more time to interact with the content.

e-Learning Architecture: Different Approaches

VCs have very specific value for "celebrity", expert type, hard to get or find person to feature. Limit VCs to these uses.

You can launch VCs as e-learning, be aware of the limits and strengths.

③ ◀ ◀ ◀ ◀◀ ◀ ◀

Virtual classroom:
WebEx, LiveMeeting, Breeze

Celebrity, lecture, meeting

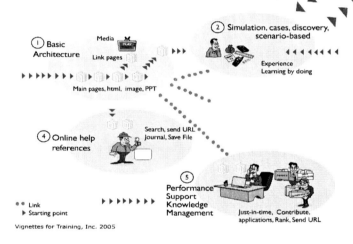

① Basic Architecture

Media

Link pages

▶▶▶

▶ ▶ ▶▶▶ ▶ ▶

Main pages, html, image, PPT

② Simulation, cases, discovery, scenario-based

◀ ◀ ◀◀ ◀◀ ◀

Experience
Learning by doing

When using VCs ideally connect them to:
Online Help & References
Basic Architecture
Simulation, cases, discovery
Performance Support and
Knowledge Management

④ Online help references

Search, send URL
Journal, Save File

⑤
Performance
Support
Knowledge
Management

Just-in-time, Contribute,
applications, Rank, Send URL

•• Link
▶ Starting point

▶ ▶ ▶▶▶ ▶ ▶

Vignettes for Training, Inc. 2005

❶ *Figure 13-1: Virtual Classrooms*

Online Reference
Help and Guide

Chapter 14

Online Reference Help and Guide

An online reference help and guide (more often called an online tutorial) is probably the most commonly used for delivery of e-Learning programs. This is the earliest generation model and continues to find its place in e-Learning programs and on the Internet (see Figure 14-1). Reference tools are knowledge repositories about a particular content subject.

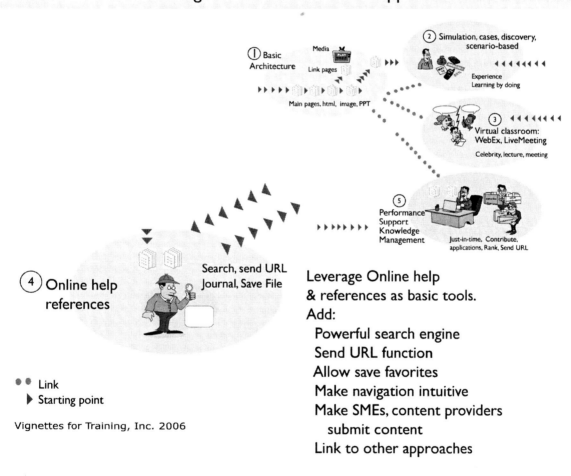

Figure 14-1: *Online Help and References*

A good reference tool:

- Allows learners to search the content.

- Provides large amounts of knowledge and data.

- Allows e-learners the capability of finding content as needed, pretty much   unconstrained. They have the freedom to randomly find what they are   looking for.

- Transfers knowledge and data quickly to dispersed learners or users.

- Allows easy, quick and inexpensive production and update.

In training we often look down on text as a way to present information and knowledge. Interestingly, why do many of us love Google?

Implementing reference tools

Successful implementations of reference tools for rapid development makes use of successful Web publishing practices.

Content and data must be published in formats that are easily searchable. This means appropriate use of HTML and XML. At the same time, there may not be a need to go through a massive writing exercise. We can leverage existing customer guides, help tips, product knowledge, marketing communications, and other information already written or prepared by writers, engineers and subject matter experts.

Add a way for learners to:

- Search the content

- Bookmark or save the pages in their favorites or commonly used list

- Forward the link page to another person

- Categorize the content based on importance or according to date.

These functions may require some programming. In addition, develop an intuitive navigation system to make it easy for learners to identify and access the knowledge. Design each specific page so links can be made to a lesson, program or other e-Learning element for easy reference.

Publish using a Content Management System (CMS) so non-technical people can construct, add, edit and update HTML pages by using WYSIWYG functions. SMEs can publish content directly to the reference material, since it is easy to use. You may also use basic publishing applications such as MS FrontPage, Macromedia Dreamweaver or Contribute.

Check out the example of a basic reference and online help: **www.vignettestraining.com.**

Performance Support Systems and Knowledge Management

Chapter 15

Performance Support Systems and Knowledge Management

Support systems used in e-Learning include performance support systems (PSS) and knowledge management systems (KM), which are usually deployed in conjunction with integrated and systems-wide implementations of large software applications and processes (see Figure 15-1).

e-Learning Architecture: Different Approaches

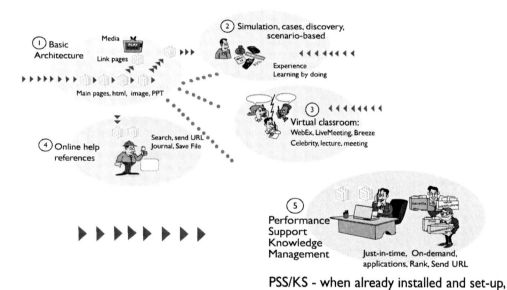

① Basic Architecture
Media
Link pages

Main pages, html, image, PPT

② Simulation, cases, discovery, scenario-based

Experience
Learning by doing

③ Virtual classroom:
WebEx, LiveMeeting, Breeze
Celebrity, lecture, meeting

④ Online help references

Search, send URL
Journal, Save File

⑤ Performance Support Knowledge Management

Just-in-time, On-demand, applications, Rank, Send URL

PSS/KS - when already installed and set-up, is best suited to support rapid e-Learning programs.
Apply and learn from PSS/KM in:
  Content submission
  Ranking of relevance
  Bookmarking/Sending URLs, Federated search
  Quick access, Just-in-time features
  Collaboration through WIKIs, blogs, podcasting, etc.

•• Link
▶ Starting point

Vignettes for Training, Inc. 2006

 Figure 15-1: Performance Support and Knowledge Management Systems

Salient features of performance support and knowledge management systems

Both PSS and KM are closely related to traditional training and reference systems, and for this reason they provide important architectural support to e-Learning. Among their most important features are these:

Depending on your goals and which areas of the PSS/KM implementation phases you are in, PSS/KMs can serve well for Rapid e-Learning.

- KM systems enable both learners and subject matter experts (SMEs) to contribute content. This facilitates content building and updating; and provides for more timely and relevant content, such as best practices and success experiences (tacit knowledge).

- PSS usually deliver "lesson-type" training and more in-depth programs are available to learners who want them.

- PSS deliver just-in-time or just-in-need training. Links to small topics can be added to specific performance areas.

- KM allows for advanced searches – an important feature since learners may have to look for information in massive databases.

- KM systems often enable learners, SMEs, coaches, and managers to send out URL links by e-mail, making it simple to share information.

- Both KM and PSS may allow for discussions with co-learners, mentors and coaches for exchanging messages and e-mail alerts, and for journaling or note taking.

- KM systems frequently allow ranking of content. This lets the system present pages and subjects according to relevance.

- KM provides for easy collaboration and sharing, making a good resource for work teams.

- KM is scalable and can integrate with enterprise resource planning (ERP) systems and customer relationship management (CRM) production and marketing systems.

- PSS is popular for product roll-outs, system-wide software implementations such as SAP, Oracle, etc., and for business processes, sales support and customer support.

Key weaknesses of most PSS/KMs in rapid development

Notwithstanding their outstanding features, designers must remember that PSS and KM systems have important limitations:

- PSS/KMs lack the LMS features for tracking, certification, curriculum structure, assessments, etc., and may not support transfer of this information.

- Although you can purchase them in smaller versions or by modules, many PSS/KMs require high upfront cash outlays.

- To implement PSS/KMs requires key changes in some business processes, as well as in the attitudes and culture of top management and staff. It usually takes longer to implement these systems.

- PSS/KMs may not be a rapid development solution if we are in the initial phase and just setting up the software. PSS/KMs require integrated systems. Depending on our goals and which areas of the implementation phases we are in, they can serve well for rapid development. If our PSS/KM is in place, we may use it rapidly.

Using PSS and KM systems for Rapid e-Learning development

PSS/KMs provide performance support. Unlike most e-Learning programs that are designed for lesson and classroom-like learning (focusing on retention rather than application), PSS/KMs enable users and learners to access knowledge quickly. The quicker they can access knowledge or information, the more likely they will use it.

To increase the quality experience of our e-Learning programs, we must incorporate:

- Quick access to content

- Sending out e-mails with URLs and links

- Lesson pages or content pages linked for specific subjects

- Powerful search options

- Ranking the relevance of pages

To increase speed of development, we must incorporate:

- Content submission from SMEs, learners, coaches (CMS or use of Contribute)

Learning Management Systems (LMS) and Learning Content Management Systems (LCMS)

Chapter 16

Learning Management Systems (LMS) and Learning Content Management Systems (LCMS)

Learning Management Systems (LMSs) primarily provide registration, database storage of activities, tracking and reporting via databases. They are largely used for tracking. They do not provide an e-Learning Architecture, even though many vendors claim that an LMS *is* an architecture. Yes, it is, from a software point of view, but not from a learning point of view.

The "C" in LCMS means that the LMS has the capability to optimize content by easy reuse and easy reproduction and management. The content management goal is to cut the development time and decrease costs since much of the content can be reused or reconstructed from existing databases of programs, graphics, audio and video files, references, etc. In other words, the "C" -- when managed well -- is capable of making the e-Learning cycle more rapid : minimum 3-minutes to ingest lesson, impetus to apply the snippet of knowledge and skill just learned, and get the targeted performance result!

> *LMSs are largely administrative tools. We need to be creative and demand more from our vendors to provide those LMS features and functions that facilitate or improve learning.*

Traditional LMSs focus on data processing and are weak in supporting e-Learner needs

Typically, an LMS does not provide an e-Learning Architecture. This is unfortunate since an LMS has great potential not only to provide tracking but also to help in promoting a better way to learn for e-learners. Most LMSs are codified practices and migration of the old classroom-like tracking of attendees.

LMSs tend to focus on registration, monitoring attendance, testing, certification and training reporting for completion of classes. They provide little impact on actually meeting e-learners' needs. Largely, LMSs are administrative tools, not learning tools.

LMSs are for tracking, not for content development – they cause integration delays

LMSs are strong in tracking and participant management functions, but very weak in helping developers construct e-Learning lessons and programs. Much of the content is developed using authoring software external to LMSs. The content developer and the IT person must integrate the content into the LMS. This integration process is a cause for delays in implementing e-Learning programs.

The integration of LMSs and content programs is usually the most treacherous part of e-Learning development. It takes too much time.

LMSs purchased, acquired, and maintained by IT or MIS are prone to delays caused by "silos" or "interdepartmental politics"

In many instances, IT acquires the LMS without the input or influence of e-Learning or training professionals. Therefore, the choice meets the IT standards, but not the rapid development requirements of training departments. An even more difficult situation occurs when the e-Learning implementation and administration functions are so segregated that it takes weeks to pass jobs back and forth between IT and the training department.

What could take 30 minutes to implement will often require two or more weeks to complete!

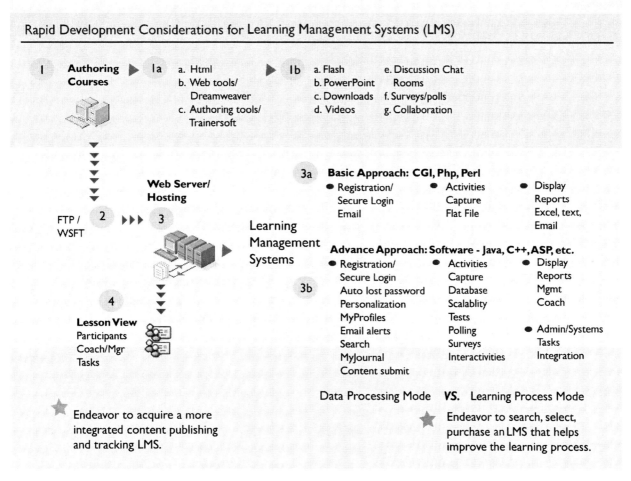

Figure 16-1: Learning Management Systems

LMSs have a strategic procurement life-cycle; once acquired, they can stay with us for 10 years or more

Acquiring an LMS is a major capital outlay. So, when it is acquired, the LMS may have to stay with our organization for quite a few years. It is difficult to replace an LMS due to the investment in time and hours, process of integration and costs.

How can we work around or maximize our LMS for Rapid e-Learning?

We could negotiate or plan with IT to work around or share responsibility for the LMS, which enables us to have full access to functions of the LMS (see Figure 16-1).

We could seek authorization and control to:

- Manage registration.

- Have a test server or test site so we can publish and test our content quickly.

- Suspend, delete and publish programs.

- Send out notices or communicate with our participants.

- Generate reports.

- Manage and change participant information for technical or user support.

The more we manage and have access to the LMS, the more readily we can deploy programs using our LMS. If our rapid development project is required in a few days or few weeks, and IT has constraints or is unwilling to share responsibilities over the management of the LMS, we should agree in advance with IT about hiring a third party LMS provider to host our programs for the purposes of rapid deployment. Then, at a given time, we may move or migrate these programs or link the data of participant activities to our internal LMS. On the other hand, we may opt to link these programs to our LMS later on. It would help for IT to approve this vendor or provider and to conduct a study of the third party capabilities and compatibilities with our LMS.

This approach is happening in many situations. For example, we may want to deploy our programs by using WebEx or LiveMeeting since our need is urgent. We may then link the program with our LMS for tracking purposes. We may also hire services like Brainshark for displaying our PowerPoint presentations, and then link these to our programs in the LMS later.

In selecting an LMS, we should find one that has more integrative functions between the content development and tracking – a Rapid Assembly LMS. For example, there are LMSs that allow you develop content in the LMS. In a matter of hours you can complete and delivery your Rapid e-Learning program.

Get involved in the requirements gathering and purchase of an LMS. Be involved in the strategic decision-making and make sure the LMS can support future Rapid
e-Learning development efforts. Select an LMS that provides more functions to support the quality of the programs.

When all else fails, and the LMS, the IT department, or the staff says, "We can't publish tomorrow or next day or next week," be a "guerilla e-trainer." If you must, publish the content in a Web site or Intranet, by-passing an LMS.

In some companies, divisions or departments that require rapid delivery of e-Learning programs will negotiate and get an agreement with IT that they retain a hosted or for-lease LMS aside from the corporate LMS. The hosted LMS is dedi-

Learning Management System

Integrated   Seamless

Rapid e-Learning: Software Reusability and Rapid Production Process

Chapter 17

Rapid e-Learning: Software Reusability and Rapid Production Process

So far I have presented here different approaches to e-Learning architectures. My main purpose has been to provide a foundation for making informed and better decisions based on design, processes, software and implementation. The lack of a well-defined e-Learning Architecture is the major cause of slow implementation, high costs and ineffective programs. On the other hand, a well thought-out e-Learning Architecture leads to an efficient way of coordinating SMEs, software producers and developers, graphic artists, writers and managers. It is also a way to persuade our senior management to take a new look at our 3-Minute e-Learning programs.

Reusability is a business goal. Oftentimes, developers are not aware of this need until project managers or business managers add this as a requirement.

In the succeeding parts, I will focus on two points: first, I'll describe how to leverage authoring software and delivery applications for high **reusability** and rapid development. I'll conclude by explaining how to hasten the **development process** of production through collaboration.

As a review, Figure 17-1 below shows the different components or methods of an e-Learning Architecture.

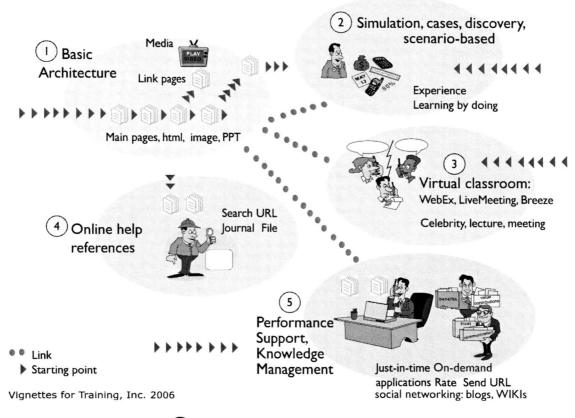

e-Learning Architecture: Different Approaches

Vignettes for Training, Inc. 2006

Figure 17-1: An e-Learning Architecture is made up of a variety of components or methods.

There are too many software applications supporting these components that to mention or illustrate all of them here. However, here is a summary and some examples of the software that supports each method within the e-Learning Architecture:

Basic architecture. Usually these are applications intended for basic content presentation. Some examples are PowerPoint, HTML editors such as Dreamweaver & FrontPage, Adobe PDF, Word documents, Excel files, Photoshop and Fireworks for graphics, Real Media and MS Media Player for audio, and MPEG or QuickTime for video. Authoring software like Lectora and OutStart may also be classified in this category.

Simulation, cases, discovery, scenario-based. Interactive design tools for simulation are Flash, Captivate, SimWriter.

Virtual classroom. Hosted tools include WebEx, LiveMeeting, Elluminate, and Breeze.

Online help references. These would include CMS (content management system), WIKI modules, and applications that support "frequently asked questions" (FAQs).

Performance support, knowledge management. Systems applications that can be used are XML, HTML, CMS, LMS, KM and server-driven applications.

Each method shown in Figure17-1 uses one or a combination of these applications. Some software have universal use. For example, HTML editors and graphics tools are used in all of the methods. Other software are specific to a method, for example, WebEx or Breeze for virtual classroom.

A Game Plan for Selection of Rapid Development Software

Chapter 18

A Game Plan for Selection of Rapid Development Software

The cornerstones of Rapid e-Learning, including 3-Minute e-Learning, design and development are: e-Learning Architecture (e-LA), content design, software utilization, and the development process.

> We need to have a software game plan or utilization plan that meets our rapid, even 3-minute, development objectives.
>
> The game plan must support our e-LA and content design and it should achieve our goals in e-Learning design and development.

As we develop this software game plan for rapid development, we will need to address the following issues:

- **Business needs**: Will the software solutions meet the organization's needs rapidly, with some balance for mid-term and long term concerns? We don't want to implement rapid solutions only to find that we incur huge costs in the long run.

- **Quality**: Regardless of the urgency, will we meet e-Learner needs? Although this outcome is often taken for granted in rapid development, producers must verify that Rapid e-Learning will support 3-Minute e-Learning, rapid application and learning.

- **Content design:** Will the authoring and delivery software allow the design to persist in the final product? It is common to see creative learning designs that are cut short or not supported by the software. In essence, does the software compromise the quality?

- **Integration:** Will we have the fastest, simplest, most wholly-integrated software that requires the least time to develop using less-complex and easy-to-learn solutions?

- **SME time:** Will the authoring software cut the time required of subject matter experts (SMEs)? Will it facilitate SME submission, sharing and approval of content?

> *Reusability is a management issue more than a software development requirement. We could say that it is a management concept applied to software development.*

- **Software dependencies:** Will the use of the software make us heavily dependent on IT talent, expertise and related services? We should find ways to control the processes, and share and collaborate with IT in the implementation of the solutions.

- **Affordable and overall high payback**: Will the software realize the highest payback of investment in actual dollars and time? Is the cost within our budget?

- **Culture and politics:** Will the software solution appeal to divergent interests? Will it help to overcome political differences or conflicting objectives that may torpedo our Rapid e-Learning initiative?

- **IT supported platforms:** Will our solutions be accepted by IT? Will they be within the boundaries of IT policy or "tolerances"? The IT department may allow some software that they do not wholly support, but an alternate support plan has to be in place.

Reusability: Project management decisions

Reusability is a management issue more than a software development requirement. We could say that it is a management concept applied to software development. One way to leverage software in e-Learning is to add management direction. In addition, some minimum understanding by trainers and developers will aid them in influencing the use of software in e-Learning. Let's look at the basic assumptions.

There are essentially three concerns in software selection: (a) the software built-in functions, which do most of the generic processing, (b) customizing the software output in order to produce specific outcomes, and (c) reusing the customized software output as a tool or utility.

Flash, Authorware and Qarbon Viewlet are examples of software with functions that let us create slide shows for a particular e-Learning project (customizing). With each of these applications, we can also create a template that allows us to reuse the slide show later in other projects. In other words, we can create our own reusable tools (the templates) with these applications and with many other similar ones.

Most developers will apply the built-in software functions in order to execute individual e-Learning tasks – for example, tracking the learner's response to a multiple-choice question. However, customization requires more planning and creative thinking and is often a more challenging task.

Customization is how we get tailored, customized and specific desired results. Yet most developers, as users of software, do not find it simple to customize the software output to meet the outcome. Furthermore, thinking of reusability is the least of their concerns. This is where we need a good project manager or an e-Learning champion in order to add the "business sense" or "management sense" to the process. Rapid e-Learning development is mainly a business consideration in software selection. The decision to build, use and reuse templates, tools and utilities is made by the e-Learning project manager, champion or leader.
Reusability is a business decision more than an IT or design decision.

As an example of another challenge in software selection, when we purchase a Learning Management System (LMS), programmers or specialists in our IT department will make it work using the built-in and standard key functions and features. However, they usually stop there. If we present them with a unique challenge, where the solution is not apparent, we might encounter resistance. Usually trainers and non-techies, unfamiliar with technology, will readily accept the reasons provided at face value. These reasons may sound like "these are systems limitations of the software", "it's costly to configure," or "it will take time to customize the functions." More often than not, there are work-arounds or simple adjustments or minor customizations that could achieve our goal. In fairness to the IT professionals, project managers often do not provide them enough time to create new ways to apply the software. The IT department is always loaded with tons of work.

This issue is a key problem in using software for e-Learning: the lack of creative use of the software to produce even higher-quality results.

Reusability involves the following concepts and benefits:

- Reduced time and costs

- Maximum utilization

- Mass production

- Simplification

- Standardization

- Quality control

- Rapid replication

- Shorter learning curve

- Ease of use

Depending on our focus and needs in rapid e-Learning development, we may build on one or more of these benefits. In the illustration below, I will show how we can realize benefits by applying the reusability concept when developing simple interactive designs or exercises.

Rapid development techniques for software reuse

To illustrate development for reuse, let's look at authoring a reusable interactive exercise. Incidentally, these ideas are also applicable in software design for an LMS or other applications. In any Rapid e-Learning development effort our scenario or situation may change, but we will focus generally on the same few key areas to control and manage the project.

Begin by identifying some possible goals and scenarios for the reusable interactive exercise:

- **Goal**: Reduce the cost, increase the speed of development and simplify the process.
  Scenario: We plan to implement the same type of interactivity dozens of times but we feel that our development approach is too cumbersome, it involves too many steps and is really slow. The developer customizes every version.

- **Goal:** Enable non-technical staff to develop, update and create content.
  Scenario: We have several staff members to help with our urgent needs, but they only have basic software skills. Right now, only the developer is able to customize the exercise.

- **Goal:** Maintain consistent style and methods.
  Scenario: Our trainers are all creative and their designs are inconsistent from one exercise to the next. This delays approval and also slows down the process.
- **Goal:** Maintain learning instructional design and outcomes.
  Scenario: Since every trainer is developing his or her own instructional design, the results may not be consistent. The participants are learning a new instructional approach design each time.

Now, apply these goals and scenarios to the design.

Dimensions of a reusable tool

The learner's view of the interactive exercise, called The Golf Exercise, is shown in Figure 18-1 below. You can view a demonstration model of the exercise online at **www.vignettestraining.com**. I refer to this application as a reusable tool because it is designed in such a way as to allow the developer to change the content it presents so that it can be used repeatedly as new e-Learning content is being developed

This is the learner's view of the reusable game.

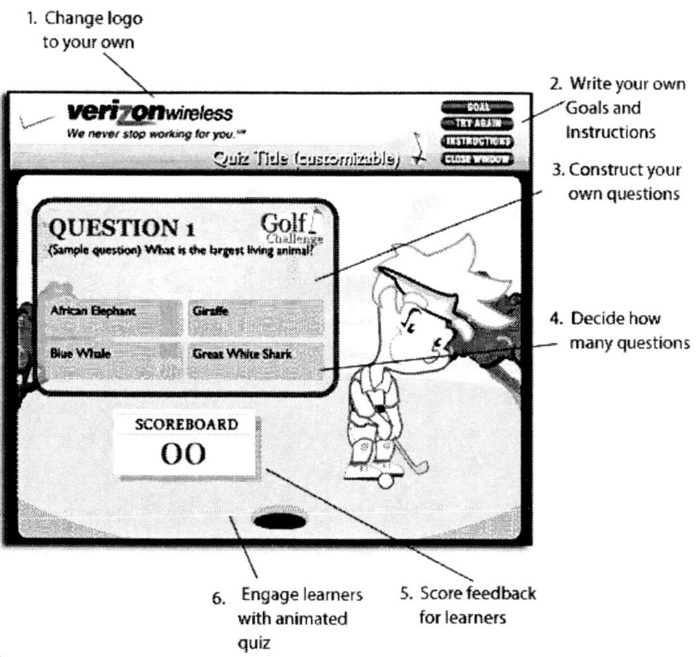

Figure 18-1: *The learner's view of The Golf Exercise, a reusable game or tool.*

In this exercise, the designer achieved reusability by separating the learner's view from the developer's or SME's view. Figure 18-2 shows the form the developer uses. The developer can enter content, change the logo, change the questions, specify the instructions and make decisions about interactivity. When the developer is finished, a single click of a "Submit" button (not shown) produces the customized exercise. The developer or SME does not have to do any programming. As a result, this exercise is reusable as often as required, without the help of a Flash developer. The content developer, writer or SME can revise the content in a matter of minutes.

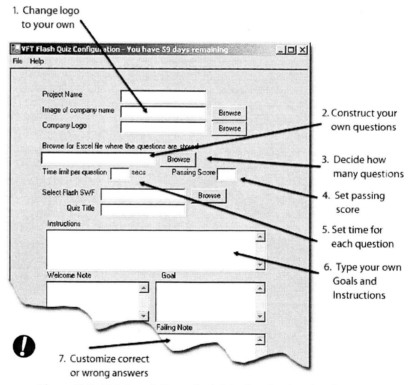

Figure 18-2: This form is the writer's interface for changing the content of the Golf Exercise.

There are essentially six functions associated with a reusable tool design, depending on purpose and complexity (in this case a basic interactive exercise). Each function offers an opportunity for rapid development. The functions are: content entry, aesthetics, interactive engine, navigation, software coding and database integration.

Content entry

We create lessons, quizzes, exercises, feedback, evaluation, etc., mostly by entering content, knowledge or ideas in the form of text. If we plan to use an exercise design a dozen or even hundreds of times and in different programs, content entry is where a lot of "new" and "repeating effort" is required. This is also where many of our SMEs and developers will enter content, and it is an ideal opportunity to reduce time, effort and costs.

To aid in Rapid e-Learning development, the template or reusable tool should allow content writers, SMEs, proofreaders and editors to add, delete, revise and update the text component of the template or the tool.

In Figure 18-1, the instructions, the goals of the exercise and the questions are provided by an SME, a content developer or a trainer. These are items 2 and 3 in Figure 18-1. In Figure 18-2, callout item 2 indicates that the SME would enter the questions in an Excel spreadsheet. Callout item 6 in Figure 18-2 shows where the content developer or a trainer enters the text for the goals and instructions.

Aesthetics

Art design, color palettes, font styles, illustration or photo design, look and feel and any "eye- candy" are included under this heading.

We can divide the creative look and feel into: (a) universal or generic to the total program or company or (b) specific to the content. In many cases the generic aesthetics (logo, colors, program titles, etc.) can be a one-time effort. We can add aesthetics for specific content or programs specifically as they are needed. By doing this, our reusable tool or template reduces the strain on our creative staff since they will change only the specific design to match the topic, rather than continually redoing the entire generic design. The reusable tool should be simple enough to allow non-technical graphics people to get a new graphic and add it to the reusable tool.

Usually a graphics designer constructs the aesthetic elements, but the ideas come from the content writer and SME. To some extent, content writers can change colors, themes, skins and backgrounds to vary the themes while allowing consistency of these from program to program. Photos and illustrations are best done by creative and graphic artists and published in a common resource library that everyone can access at any time. In this case, we may also ask the trainers and even SMEs to add this graphic even though they possess only very basic skills. We can even provide reusable graphics so they don't need to invent a new one.

In Figure 18-2, notice that the developer can specify only the image of the company name, the logo and the quiz title. Other graphic elements are fixed within the Flash movie, discussed below under "Software coding."

Interactive engine

Interactivity, especially in games and exercises, increase the discovery, experiential and emotional impact of the exercise.

Content writers and SMEs influence heavily the interactive design. For example, SMEs or content writers design a game or exercise in listening skills or time management. However, the interaction engineer does the execution and the interactive engineering. Interactive engineers are hard to find since their talent is a mix between content development in training and experience in film making, advertising, gaming and discovery processes. Programming the exercise is also a higher-level skill that one does not often find in trainers, SMEs or developers.

Another good example might be a reusable tool for designing maze exercises. Such an exercise allows the learner to follow different paths to discover answers to a case or a scenario. Creating an "engine" (or programming tool) to generate a reusable maze game may require varied skills and a lot of time investment. However, if we plan to reuse the exercise in numerous programs, we may consider creating a tool to handle the heavy lifting. Although programmers will develop the engine, the tool allows the trainer or developer to select or construct the maze options and enter the content in each box of the maze. The trainer builds the content choices, without having to call the programmer to add the boxes. The trainer or SME can simply publish, edit and redo the maze boxes, their content and various options until the exercise goals are achieved.

This concept also applies in creating reusable tools for randomizing tests, creating different types of questions, conducting surveys and publishing content online.

The key concept is that even in complex designs, entering content and data can be facilitated if we focus on isolating those activities that change from version to version, and make it easy for non-technical people to use the tool. In other words, make as reusable as possible those parts which often cause delays and require constant change or entry by many people. Rapid development is one key advantage, but cost control is also a major benefit. We will use less expensive programmer's time. In our examples in Figures 18-1 and 18-2, the only active element set by the programmer is the time limit per question.

Navigation

Navigation includes interface elements that enable learners to control the tool and the presentation, e.g. forward and back buttons, links, start or begin button, etc. Usually navigation in software is permanent, fixed and standardized. While this area is less reusable, the text, colors, backgrounds, buttons and graphics in the buttons are (or should be) customized to match the aesthetics of your exercise. The behavior and functions of the navigation elements are usually not reusable. They can be, but the cost is high and usually impacts the entire design of the software, not just the reusable tool.

Navigation elements in Figure 18-1 are limited, and include the "Try Again" and "Close Window" buttons. The developer has no control over the behavior of these controls.

Software coding

Software codes, created by the programmers and the software architect, run the reusable tool. Whether we purchase or build our own software, for authoring or for an LMS, we have the ability to influence the direction by making sure that the software is able to help in rapid development. Make it a requirement that it is easy or inexpensive to use to develop reusable tools, or it has many built-in reusable features.

As we can see in Figure 18-2, the developer's form allows the designer or the developer to choose the Flash movie (SWF) to be used with the exercise. A Flash developer, separate from the rest of the team, creates the movie.

Database integration

Data collection and integration to database and reporting functions are deep programming issues best left to database developers and managers. Since our reusable tool may have to access the database, this area is usually affected when we design software and reusable tools.

Process and Collaboration for 3-Minute e-Learning Development

Chapter 19

Process and Collaboration for 3-Minute e-Learning Development

Major deficiencies that slow down e-Learning development are the lack of a collaborative electronic tool and failure to develop a collaborative culture and norm among the members of the team.

Josh Bersin of Bersin & Associates states that the typical e-Learning production mode is like the "waterfall" process for software development. It is linear, and proceeds in typical mass production-line fashion in which each part of the product goes step-by-step from start to completion.

Rapid development is possible with the use of online collaboration and project management tools. This saves time by faster decision-making.

With the linear production process (one step at a time), programs are developed slowly. By contrast, the collaborative method is a parallel and simultaneous process –with tasks being done almost at the same time.

Conditions contributing to success of collaboration in Rapid e-Learning

To support parallel and collaborative production, two things must occur: (1) the culture and attitudes of the team members must be cooperative and must encourage teamwork and open communication, and (2) the team should be using collaborative software.

Collaborative software brings about these results:

- Increases the speed of coordination

- Eliminates paperwork

- Hastens real-time sharing of results

- Facilitates feedback

- Speeds up decision-making

- Organizes documentation and version controls

- Improves controls of the minute details

- Clarifies accountability

Key features of collaboration software to support rapid development

Collaborative software is a Web-based application accessible to all team members 24/7.

Central location

Most collaboration tools are centralized, allowing the exchange of information among members in one or numerous locations, globally or locally. A Web-based system allows greater flexibility. Users can simply log on to the Internet from anywhere and retrieve information from a single Web address.

Organization is key

With the great amount of information available, and multiple users having access to the collaboration tool, it is necessary to create categories (i.e., folders by topic, groups, etc.) to avoid confusion. For instance, we can place minutes of meetings in a conference folder while presentations slated for review may be placed in another folder, with different fields identifying the particular version.

Real-time updates

A tracker feature allows participants or users to submit tasks, problems or issues that may be addressed to a particular person or group. These range from technical queries or updates to suggestions for improvement, as well as site or project rectifications.

Notification

More important, the person who is best suited to address the problem is notified.

Discussion room

An online discussion room provides the venue for the exchange of ideas and opinions as well as brainstorming for new ones. Users can post ideas, introduce new topics or cases for a fresh outlook, and ask questions to get answers about problems. A manager, team leader or coach can lead these discussions so team members can engage in candid and open discussions over issues.

File retrieval

A collaboration tool eliminates the need to store files in one place while keeping an online discussion in another. Thus, during discussions or reviews, one can immediately access the file needed for reference or upload a new version through a simple file transfer feature. From documents to spreadsheets, slide shows, audio and even video files, all can be uploaded and retrieved from one location.

Access to helpful information

Think of the collaboration tool as one huge library filled with bookshelves and filing cabinets. All the information we use are in the cabinets, while all the reference information needed are on the bookshelves. A collaboration tool can host valuable reference materials, even online programs and templates, which may be necessary for our respective e-Learning programs. Links to various references may be provided, e.g. prototypes, templates, demos and examples.

Issue tracker

As our e-Learning program makes progress, there will be a great number of minute details to be attended to, for example, typos, color changes, etc. These are small details, but you have to address them. The issue tracker is a collaborative feature, so everyone can post issues and track progress. The issue tracker notifies whoever is responsible; he or she can make updates to it, and it alerts the person asking or directing the change. This method ensures that all details are taken care of.

Job Aids for the Development Team

Chapter  20

Job Aids for the Development Team

Two tables in this book can assist us in Rapid e-Learning development, particularly our 3-Minute e-Learning.

Production processes and schedule

In Rapid e-Learning, there are many opportunities to increase the speed of development and to eliminate traps that leads to high costs. Please review Table 20-1. The last column identifies areas for Rapid e-Learning development.

Rapid e-Learning development decisions

Sometimes it is not clear whether taking a rapid approach to e-Learning development will be beneficial or not. Table 20-2 presents a number of considerations and a scoring system that will help us to make a "go/no-go" decision.

Suggestions on how best to use the Rapid e-Learning Development and Management Decision Aid

One of the challenges in implementing Rapid e-Learning is to educate internal or external clients on its best use. Oftentimes, clients see Rapid e-Learning from a limited point of view. They can see the benefits and the potentials to alleviate the pressures for instant delivery of knowledge and learning. This is positive. But on the other hand, this may also cause severe problems because expectations are not realistic.

To help internal or external clients make good decisions, we must use the decision aid as part of the process.

These are the suggested steps:

1. When a client asks to implement a Rapid e-Learning program, we must first call for a project review meeting. The purpose of the meeting is for our team and the client to assess how best to meet the needs.

2. We may send in advance a copy of the decision aid (Table 20-2) with a cover email suggesting a preliminary review of the need be made by going through the checklist. The objective of the meeting is to develop a good strategy.

3. At the meeting, we must go through the decision aid point-by-point. We use the decision aid as a questionnaire for the client and the team.

4. The scoring presented in the decision aid allows our team and the client to realize the different issues involved in the decisions.

5. The answers to the questions also help us formulate a plan which includes how to meet challenges and maximize opportunities.

6. The meeting helps the client see the different aspects of the Rapid e-Learning project. They also see the challenges of procuring resources and information to make the project happen.

In one meeting or several, the client will either reinforce its need for Rapid e-Learning or they will opt to use another method of delivery. Either way, we must help our client make a sound decision.

Table 20-1 Rapid e-Learning production issues Phase/Task	Resources	Comments for Rapid e-Learning considerations (italics)
Project Initiation Phase • needs analysis, readiness & viability studies, strategy formulation and proposal development • conducting a rapid e-Learning review (see checklist references) • project approval • kick-off meeting		*Quickly determine rapid e-Learning requirements and qualifications; get approval that this project falls under rapid development.*
Content & Systems Planning Phase • **design** • **features & functions**		
Design e-Learning document development	SME, ID, Mgr. Interactive	*Agree with your team on the documentation and collaboration tools and processes to use.*
Design document review	Dir. Development	
Contractual design document	Management, ID	*Involve the legal department early, if needed. They require more time than others.*
Write (outline) content based on e-Learning design	SME	*Educate SMEs, control interviews with guided questions and provide template questions or tools.*
Analyze/clarify/distill/categorize content	Writer	*Educate and guide.*
QA e-Learning design, content review	Editor	*Use models, templates, produce prototypes for quick approvals.*
Graphic, theme, interactive design requirements	Art Director	*Educate and guide.*
Interactive design and content plan review	Mgr. Interactive	*Educate and guide.*
Finalizing systems & LMS features	Developer	*Involve IT early. Negotiate for an exemption.*
Review design/plan, review/approval to client	Management	*Use models, templates, produce prototypes for quick approvals.*

Table 20-1 Rapid e-Learning production issues (continue)		
Phase/Task	**Resources**	**Comments for Rapid e-Learning considerations (italics)**
Project Phase • storyboard • assembly and testing		*Use your approved architecture.*
Develop storyboard	Instructional Technologist Mgr. Interactive, Art Director	*Use models, templates. Develop a rapid storyboard by using outline content format with references to standard style in graphics and interactivities.*
Create graphics and interactivities	Art Director, Program Developer	*Use reference library and clearly state style expectations. Prepare creative briefs for standards.*
Storyboard review	SME	*Get consent from SMEs that they follow your content development architecture and that changes will occur quickly by involving them in the collaboration process and use of the software.*
Storyboard review/revision	Project Lead	
Editing	Editor	*Start this early with SME content submission.*
Evaluation/adjustment	Management	
Integration of content to database and other software	Program Developer	*Plan ahead for this. Test by IT the type of integration challenges you may face. Test ahead of time.*
Permission/producing graphics	Dir. Development	*Avoid using photos not within the creative briefs. Securing and looking for photos takes time. Ask artists to search for photos as concepts are developed in the content. Ensure writers provide clear image guides.*
Revision of graphics/interactivities	Graphic Designer, Program Developer	
Final assembly	Program Developer	*Test final assembly by doing prototypes. Don't wait for your project content to be finished and then test with LMS and other components.*
Proofreading	Proofreader	*Do early in the process. Have a proofreader in writing stage.*
Testing and prototype delivery	Program Developer	*Do a prototype at the earliest time possible. Focus on prototyping all key decisions to be made since decisions may hinder speed in development.*
Review	ID, SME, Project Lead	*Review is in every step of the process, not at a final point.*

Table 20-1 Rapid e-Learning production issues (continued)		
Phase/Task	Resources	Comments for Rapid e-Learning considerations (italics)
Testing/Release Phase • alpha release • beta release • version 1.0 course launch		
Alpha version review	Management	*Construct prototypes to cut time. Use alpha and beta testing.*
Client review	Management	*Involve clients, target users ahead of the timeframes and seeks agreement that their review is on progression of completion of programs, not when the program is done. Focus on small and constant reviews.*
Post-client evaluation (if necessary)	Management Project Lead	
Implementation of client changes	Program Developer	*Agree in the kickoff meeting to rigid change policies and procedures. Avoid changes at all costs and get agreement on what types of changes are show stoppers or minor changes, which may be done in later versions.*
First round of functional QA	Tester	*Assign testers as separate people, not the writers, software developers or others doing the developing.*
Implementation of QA changes	Program Developer	
Build Beta version	Management	
Second round of functional QA	Tester	
Regressive QA	Proofreader, ID	*This is always a must to focus on. Rapid development requires that you pay attention to software and parts of your program that must be reviewed for consistency and functionality, especially if you're rushing and adding late features into your software.*
Version 1.0 release		
Total Development		

CONSIDERATION	INSTRUCTIONS	POINTS	ENTRY
Table 20-2 *Rapid e-Learning development management consideration decision aid*			
Number of Learners	If there are: Fewer than 50 50 to 100 More than 100	0 5 10	
Distance of learners from existing training site	If bringing the average learner to an existing site: Does not require an overnight stay Does require an overnight stay Requires many overnight stays	0 5 10	
Software in place and trained staff	If software is in place and staff trained: No Intermediate Experienced	0 5 10	
Number of times this training program will be offered	If learners require training: Only once Two to five times Six to 19 times 20 times or more	0 3 5 10	
Frequency of updates	If changes/updates will be needed: Six months or more Between three and six months Every three months or less	0 5 10	
Development time available	If training must be available in: Three months or more Between one to three months Less than one month	0 5 10	
Preferred learning style	If learners prefer: Classroom-like learning which is controlled by lectures and traditional models Virtual Classroom - lecture online Fast-paced learning where they can take control based on their need to perform faster	0 5 10	
Availability of e-Learning Architecture	Is a sound e-Learning Architecture for this type of project/design already in place: No Yes	0 10	
Preferred training schedule	If it is more appropriate to: Set training schedules Mix Allow learners to set schedules	3 5 10	
Openness of Subject Matter Experts to e-Learning Architecture	Are your SMEs open to the idea of having an e-Learning Architecture to aid in the rapid development of e-Learning programs? No Maybe Yes	0 3 10	
Current computer proficiency	If learners: Do not know how to use a PC and do not need one in their job Do not know how to use a PC but need one on their job Know how to use a computer	0 5 10	

Table 20-2 *Rapid e-Learning development management consideration decision aid*

CONSIDERATION	INSTRUCTIONS	POINTS	ENTRY
Software Skills	If SMEs and e-trainers: Do not have basic skills in contributing through software Know how to use PowerPoint, HTML, Dreamweaver, Front Page, Adobe PDF and MS Word and Excel for basic content development Know how to run media development and tools such as Flash, Authorware, etc. for interactive design.	0 5 10	
Current learner skill level	If learners: Have widely varying skill levels Have varying skills All have the same skill level	0 5 10	
Need for individualized remediation	If learners: Will likely need remediation Will likely not need remediation	0 10	
Application of knowledge (learning outcomes)	If the staff: Is required to apply knowledge primarily for retention, completion and certification processes Is required to apply knowledge and skills instantly in their particular tasks Is required to obtain knowledge only	0 5 10	
Consistency	If consistency of instruction is: Very important Somewhat important Not important	0 5 10	
Content already available on e-Learning format	If e-Learning program: Must be developed to meet requirements Can be purchased and modified to meet needs Can be purchased without modification	0 5 10	
Availability of content	If content is: Not available - still has to be researched and built from scratch Partially available - existing content still needs to be revised/add new information that still has to be researched Available and "must learn" critical content already identified	0 5 10	
Type of content	If skills are: Interpersonal Technical Knowledge	0 5 10	
Management's past experience with e-Learning	If past experience was: Not favorable Neutral Very favorable Neutral	0 5 10 5	

CONSIDERATION	INSTRUCTIONS	POINTS	ENTRY
Table 20-2 *Rapid e-Learning development management consideration decision aid*			
Past experience in dealing with Subject Matter Experts (SMEs)	Based on previous dealings with SMEs, were they: Not readily available and uncooperative Cooperative, but difficult to schedule meetings with Always available and cooperative	0 5 10	
General view of technology	If management views computer technology as: Awful A necessary evil Great	0 5 10	
Budgeting scheme	For cost comparisons. If development costs: Are separated from the cost fo delivery Are included with delivery cost	0 10	
Availability of hardware at learner site	If hardware at learner site is: Not available Available but needs upgrading Available, no upgrade required	0 5 10	
Learning Management System (LMS) or Learning Content Management System (LCMS) and Integration in place	Is a Learning Management System already existing and in place? No Yes	0 10	
Budget situation	If cash funding is: Slow Adequate Good	0 5 10	
Access to Learning Management System (LMS)	If the control and access to a Learning Management System: Limited to the IT team Can be shared with other members of the development team Is managed and operated by designers, trainers who must implement e-learning e-Learning	0 5 10	
Management's perception of person making the e-Learning recommendation	If person making the recommendation: Has a poor track record Has a fair track record Has a successful track record	0 3 10	
Work environment and culture	Is the work environment inclined to support collaboration among team members: Not at all Neutral Yes	0 5 10	
Availability and skills of project management staff	If staff can: Not adequately manage rapid development of an e-Learning program Manage this type of project with relative ease	0 10	
Availability of production hardware and supplies	If production hardware and supplies are: Not available Partially available but needs upgrade Not needed Available	0 3 5 10	

Table 20-2 *Rapid e-Learning development management consideration decision aid*

CONSIDERATION	INSTRUCTIONS	POINTS	ENTRY

Availability of templates and content development tools	If templates and content development tools are:
	    Not available
	    Partially available but needs extensive
	      modifications
	    Immediately available and can easily be
	      reused for other projects
		0
		
		5
		
		10	

Availability, knowledge and capability of staff in designing and authoring tools/language	If staff:
	    Does not know anything about designing and
	      authoring
	    Can outsource the process quickly, given that
	      staff capabilities and resources are
	      insufficient for rapid development
	    Can design and author e-Learning programs
	      rapidly
		0
		
		5
		
		10	

Availability of hardware troubleshooter/quality control	If troubleshooters:
	    Cannot be made available
	    Can be made available
		5
		10	

Availability of Subject Matter Experts	If content questions must be answered and experts:
	    Cannot be made available on site
	    Can be made available on site
		5
		10	

Use of existing trainers	If trainers now on staff:
	    Will no longer be needed
	    Can be transferred to a new position
	    Can be used on the Rapid e-Learning projects
		0
		5
		10	

	TOTAL		

LEGEND:

1. If total is less than 180: You probably should not consider Rapid e-Learning for this project.
2. If the total is between 180 and 250: You should take a second look at the options.
3. If the total is over 300: Rapid e-Learning may be viable.

Note: This is not a scientific study. The purpose is to assist in your review of the key points in considering a Rapid e-Learning project.

Table 20-1 was adapted from the "Decision Process for e-Learning" prepared by Thomas Gafford, e-Learning Manager from Northrop Grumman.

3-Minute e-Learning and Beyond to Turbo-LMS, Rapid ADDIE and e-Learning Business

Chapter 21

3-Minute e-Learning and Beyond to Turbo-LMS, Rapid ADDIE and e-Learning Business Performance Metrics

How do our LMSs perform and help us achieve our goals? In chapter 16 I shared with you my observation that most LMSs are "data processing" tools and not "learning" tools. Furthermore, LMSs are even further removed from helping learners apply ideas to improve actual job performance or solve problems since the knowledge and skills required are needed rapidly.

So far, many of us have been so busy and preoccupied with pushing content out the door, that we have left our LMSs untapped, underutilized or not providing the right strategy and direction.

Elliott Masie, a leading thinker in learning technologies (www.masie.com), and Josh Bersin of Bersin & Associates, a leading research firm (www.bersin.com), have interesting insights about the pitfalls of our current LMSs.

In Learning TRENDS, March 21, 2006, Elliott Masie presented his "18 Wishes for an LMS!" (Reprinted from Chief Learning Officer Magazine.)

Two of Masie's wishes are relevant to our discussions here.

"Wish # 8. LMS, I want you to be more integrated with our business objectives. As we roll out new products, change our strategy, realign our workforce or add new customers, you need to be hooked into the process in real time."

"Wish # 10. LMS, I want you to handle the growing use of content at the object level. Business is moving fast and, often, the learning needs are small: just a chunk of the right content, now! Stop calling that a non-completion. It is a learning moment and a success."

Josh Bersin, in his keynote speech at the Workforce Performance 2006 Conference in Las Vegas, September 2006, reported that in the study that Bersin & Associates conducted, e-Learning had largely been rated by companies to have a high value contribution in meeting goals in compliance topic areas. However, companies rated e-Learning to have a low value contribution in its ability to impact performance in companies.

The insights above are closely related. I think that as we push our LMSs to

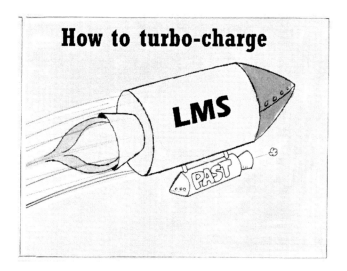

help learners use content rapidly in work situations for impacting performance or adapting skills to changes in strategies or new products, the content has to be necessarily small. "Just a chunk, content, now" as Masie says, or in our parlance, 3-Minute e-Learning. The problem, as I explained, is how do we break content into small sizes or snippets? We can't just compress bloated content or chop it into smaller lessons, while still presenting all of it. Through the 3-Minute e-Learning, Organic e-Learning Design Process (Appendix B) and the appropriate e-Learning Architecture (e-LA), I emphasized that to produce chunks of content, we have to focus on finding the application points of the content that are useful to the learner to apply rapidly on the job. It is also crucial to match the content with the right e-LA model.

3-Minute e-Learning provides a sound foundation to bridge e-Learning and knowledge content to the demands of rapid performance in actual work situations. 3-Minute e-Learning enables the learner to use the content, whether it is deployed in e-Learning 1.0, e-Learning 1.3, or e-Learning 2.0. Furthermore, 3-Minute e-Learning and the sound e-Learning Architecture (e-LA) allow us to connect knowledge with relevant job performance metrics. It is possible to see how e-Learning can really impact performance by correlating job tasks specific to 3-Minute e-Learning with critical metrics in the organization. I call this "e-Learning Business Performance Metrics. "

Let me share with you some perspectives and case examples. In the discussions below, I show that converting much of our content into 3-Minute e-Learning helps us take advantage of many advances of Learning 2.0, Web 2.0 and enhancements to LMSs. I am not suggesting that 3-Minute e-Learning is an instrumental concept before we can use the new developments in technologies. Rather, the 3-Minute e-Learning format of content facilitates our ability to use our e-Learning investment in the rapid learning mode.

I have opted to organize and present this information into three groups:

1. Facility for speed, access, collaboration and knowledge sharing
2. Rapid, real-time, dynamic, ADDIE
3. Performance metrics-driven learning

Facility for speed, access, collaboration and knowledge sharing

Online learners or those doing work using digital tools and Internet solutions exhibit e-Learning Behaviors® (Chapter 5). They prefer to have quick access to short lessons, as well as quick exits, random access, and finding solutions to solve problems and continually search for application ideas. In essence, these learners pursue what engages them or what the demands are from work situations.

e-Learning Behaviors® are even more apparent in situations where e-Learning 2.0 tools, such as WIKI, Blog, bookmarking, Instant Messaging, iPods, and others, are being used for social networking and collaboration. Since 3-Minute e-Learning is small and has stand-alone content, learners can search quickly (effective search requires that the content is tagged with the key words), bookmark their favorite lessons and email the URL (Web address) of the 3-Minute e-Learning. Additionally, learners can link the URL in WIKIs and Blogs. These behaviors are possible since the 3-Minute e-Learning content is designed to be small to allow for quick study. It is difficult to imagine online learners doing the above activities when the content is encapsulated in a large and long-winded program.

In essence, 3-Minute e-Learning facilitates these capabilities:

> • Share knowledge to help, coach or support others
quickly
>> • Share knowledge to complement formal training
>> • Access knowledge instantly to perform tasks as needed
>> • Organize learning in a very personalized manner

In "Social Life of Information" (2000), John Selly Brown observes that people and organizations lose a great amount of learning opportunities from informal sharing and networking due to the over- reliance on information technology. There is a lot of learning by people moving cubicle to cubicle and asking for ideas or solutions from other colleagues or associates. e-Learning 2.0 and Web 2.0 social computing and networking are the tools that enable people to exchange ideas instantly and informally. However, much of the knowledge being shared is experience-based and informal. Most formal learning content is not shared easily because it is difficult to search and find relevant information quickly.

Turbo-charge our LMSs: Search, bookmark favorites and email links

Although search, bookmark favorites and email link functions are common in many web based applications, most LMSs do not have these capabilities. First, these tools are against the "religions" of traditional instructional designers and trainers. They want learners to learn from A to Z in a linear fashion, the "full proficiency" model, as I mentioned earlier. Second, most e-Learning content is constructed as one solid learning media (like Flash) that makes it hard if not impossible to search the content. Thus, application points cannot be isolated for quick sharing.

If content were organized in 3-Minute e-Learning formats, the search, bookmark favorites and email link functions would make sense or become practical. We can therefore Turbo-charge our LMSs. We can make our 3-Minute e-Learning content much more accessible and realize a higher payback from our investments.

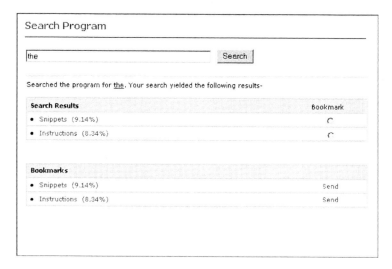

Figures 21.1 The LMS allows learners to search all programs assigned to them and bookmark topics that are of interest to them.

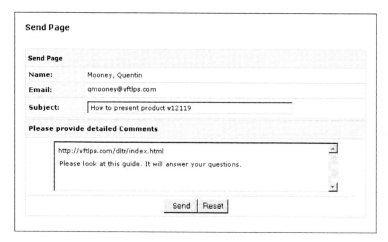

Figures 21.2 Learners are able to send an email with the URL of the bookmarked topic. Provided the recipient is registered in the system, he or she can access the bookmarked topic immediately.

Rapid, real-time, and dynamic ADDIE

Are ISD (Instructional Systems Design) and ADDIE (Analyze, Design, Develop, Implement, Evaluate) dead?

The souls of ISD and ADDIE are alive. But the body, its implementation, methods and processes are old, dead and must be buried. Many of us have abandoned ADDIE because it is cumbersome, takes too long and is costly. But the stake through ADDIE's heart is the persistent practice of rushing content development and delivery because of pressures of internal clients. "We are done with the software. Please take this week to develop the training." "We need to train 500 people in 2 weeks." "We don't have the time – Just train people on what I tell you to!"

So, OK, for now. As leaders, instructional designers, developers and trainers, we don't have much of a choice in most cases. But do we abandon ADDIE totally? Are the principles of ADDIE necessary to achieve good learning and training goals?

I believe that ADDIE is with us, alive and well. We don't recognize it as ADDIE. We don't even think of it as a valid application of ADDIE. In e-Learning 2.0, ADDIE has moved from the instructional designers' to the learners' control. Learners assess, design, develop, implement and evaluate learning. They do all of these in a rapid, real-time, as-it-happens, dynamic process. Learners constantly assess their needs on the job. They search quickly for answers and solutions in content or through other people (design and develop). Learners apply (implement) the found answers and solutions. They evaluate to see if the solution works or not. Then, they repeat the process or do a random simultaneous process. One does not know where the beginning or ending lies. What matters is that they use the content and knowledge to solve problems and get results.

This type of behavior is similar to what Masie and DiDonato call learning with your "digital tribe." While doing work in front of a computer, a worker may have Google open, 10 Instant Messaging conversations, and a reference guide ready. Or a salesperson opens her notebook in a client's office to demonstrate a point, opens her Blackberry or Treo to access the web for new pricing or to access contact information. In both cases, learning and doing are intertwined and ADDIE is actively being practiced.

Now, what is the role of 3-Minute e-Learning in Rapid ADDIE? In many of our current e-Learning designs, which are bloated with content, cumbersome and encapsulated in one file, it is impossible to efficiently use the application points of the content. In fact, no one really wants to go back to or study the e-Learning again because in the Internet high-speed world, it takes too much time. Moreover, it's inefficient to go back through the e-Learning page by page and look for the content.

Additionally, with very bloated content, we cannot provide learners a quick way of assessing the relevancy or value of the content.

To help the rapid learning demands of learners, using the illustration in Figures 21.3 and 21.4, I will show how I designed and applied in an LMS project the Ranking for Relevancy and Organic Presentation of content to learners. A fundamental assumption here is that all content is in 3-Minute e-Learning snippets, nuggets or vignettes.

This is how it works:

1. All snippets are rated by learners as to whether the content is relevant, 1 being the lowest and 10 being highly relevant (Figure 21.3);

2. The data is collected in the database.

3. With the data information stored, learners have the option to access by "Relevancy," which shows the learners the list of snippets according to relevancy and value. The LMS organically suggests or presents the ranking to the learner.

4. Learners can then study the top-rated snippets and may not bother with the low- rated ones (Figure 21.4).

In Rapid ADDIE, we are encouraging the learners to do most of the work. This is similar to what Masie refers to as adding the Amazon.com experience to our learning programs.

What does the relevancy rating provide the trainer, leader and instructional designer? It provides them the opportunity to see which topics are of high value and which ones are low. The information indicates what we may want to augment, improve, do more of or delete in the content. So, we have the chance to assess, evaluate, and, then, design and develop more content.

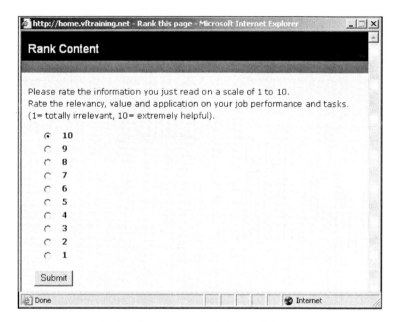

Figures 21.3 Learners rank the relevancy or usefulness of the snippet or lesson. The data is collected and compiled.

Account Management Training

High Relevancy Content

Topics	Rating 1 - 10	Rank	Raters	Best Practices	Edit/Modfiy
How to convert leads to forecasts		9	989	View	Access
How to relate forecasts to revenues		8	1210	View	Access
How to estimate income, commisions		7	876	View	Access
Developing realistic forecasts		6	450	View	Access
How to adjust, change forecasts		5	1002	View	Access
Reporting forecats to leader		4	981	View	Access
Preparing statistical analysis		3	403	View	Access
Importing forecasts from MS Project		1	201	View	Access
How to integrate CRM entries		1	322	View	Access

Figures 21.4 The ranking data is collected and presented to the learner as another option or alternative to view the 3-Minute e-Learning snippets. Learners can click "View" to study the snippet.

Performance metrics-driven learning

I personally like the new developments in e-Learning 2.0. WIKIs, Blogs, Mash-ins, Instant Messaging and others are great tools to personalize learning and increase the speed of knowledge sharing. I anticipate there will be more social networking tools in the years to come as bandwidth speed improves and portable and mobile devices become more affordable. This is truly an exciting period for training.

As I ponder these new developments, I ask this question:

"What has happened to relating e-Learning to business or organizational performance?"

Unfortunately, I see very little progress in this area.

How does 3-Minute e-Learning relate to the issue of business performance?

The case below is an example of how 3-Minute e-Learning helped in linking to or making it possible to set up e-Learning Business Performance Metrics. This was done for one of my clients, a large financial consulting firm. The client had several thousand investment advisors who needed to be continually trained.

The problems were stated as follows:

- "We don't want to waste time in training, especially unneeded training, since my staff must produce revenues of $50,000 per hour."

- "We want training that we can correlate to performance metrics and gives us a way to gauge the relationship of training and key performance indicators."

My challenge as consultant was to figure out a way to train the advisors only on what impacted measurable performance directly. The team (client, trainers and consultants) first asked the question, "What do we need to train them on?" Eventually, we realized that we were asking the wrong question. The solution became clear when we changed our question to: "What performance areas do we need to improve?" It became obvious that we needed to narrow down specific content and convert it into smaller sizes called snippets to train the advisors on the measurable areas. The idea of "training-on-need" or "training-on-exception" became the accepted principle.

In Figure 21.5, you see a screen capture of a manager's report displaying the Performance Metrics of one of the advisors. The right column displays the few key Performance Metrics. The Performance displays the measurable performance of the advisor, which is updated in real time. (The data was integrated into the LMS as it happened, collected from the in-house financial performance system.) On the left side, the related e-Learning Snippets are presented with indications of completion, timeliness, pre and post and number of attempts. Each snippet is 2-3 minutes long.

---

e-Learning and Performance Metrics   >> Back to Reports
>> Download Report

Select by Start Month ▢ | 00/00/00 | Go | Report is selected by start of Month.

New York Branch 215
Bernard Smiths AE   **Training Performance**   **Performance Metrics**

Sniplets Titles	Completion Rate	On-Time	Pre / Post	Attempts	Standards	Actual % 0 25 50 75 100 125
Lead Conversion	100%	100%	65% 95%	1	Business Assess 90%	
Assessment of Networth	95%	100%	50% 95%	3	Risk Studies 95 %	
Legal Due Dilligence	75%	100%	66% 95%	1	Returns Est $25,000	
Financial Returns Analysis	100%	95%	75% 95%	1	Dilligence 65%	
Estimation of Risks	89%	95%	70% 95%	1	Network Assess 80%	
Investigation of Assets	100%	94%	35% 95%	3		
Valuation / Appraisals	65%	93%	56% 95%	1		
Credit Reports -1	95%	90%	35% 95%	3		
	98%	75%	25% 95%	3		

Figure 21.5 The e-Learning and Performance Metrics is an enhancment of an LMS. The enhancement has been made possible because the content are in smaller snippets, 3-Minute e-Learning.

This report was presented to learners and managers alike as part of their e-Learning dashboard. The report also sent out email alerts and notices of the exceptions where learners were falling behind both in performance and recommended learning snippets. They were given recommendations for possible study. Upon viewing this report, managers were able to intervene and coach learners on both the performance issues and related learning gaps. The system also provided a coaching tool.

Managers could then generate a before-and-after report if the assigned learning helped in the performance areas. This report was known as "Snapshots of Learning Performance." It showed the variances and improvements before and after recommended learning. A correlation was done to the extent of showing how the learning snippets were helping performance. The Performance Metrics tool was an enhancement, which I introduced into the client's LMS.

The concept of correlating performance and e-Learning was made easy because there was a breakthrough in thinking. The instructional design team members radically changed their minds – converting large programs and discovering the application points for the snippets. This was a breakthrough because it took less time to build the Performance Metrics once the design and delivery of the snippets was the approach agreed on. The initial opposition to designing snippets as stand-alone almost caused the project to falter.

As a reference, we used Return on Learning, a book written by Samir Desai and his associates from Accenture (www.accenture). It is a good reference on how they tried to use Performance Metrics in learning and determining returns.

I admit that the concept of correlating training and performance in this case could be open to criticism because it did not follow the rigid data collection and analysis methodologies of formal research. The process was more a matter of gauging or making an "intelligent estimate or guess" of the correlation between learning and performance. My client was pleased with the outcome because it was practical, easy, real-time and useful, exactly what they needed. The client abhorred the suggestion of making a long, tedious, and costly ROI study, as suggested earlier in the project.

The concept of correlating e-Learning with Performance Metrics is applicable in situations where specific measurable outcomes for tasks or jobs are collected, stored and used as a day-to-day management tool. Examples are:

- Business consulting – measuring billable and non-billable hours and types of engagements

- Customer support – length of calls, speed of resolutions and complaints or repeat calls

- Sales – number of sales in pipeline, projected turnover, contract rate, applications rate, etc.

- Manufacturing – scrap rate, turnaround rate, etc.

- Healthcare – number of patients or cases managed per hour, cost of delivery of service per patient, etc.

"Provocative Innovations"

In terms of Elliott Masie's concept of "provocative innovations," it would take a head-twisting, mind-numbing and backbreaking exercise to make a change in our paradigms. But once we succeed in making the change, we discover a whole new world of possibilities. Moving away from bloated content to 3-Minute e-Learning is one of those exercises we need to pursue.

3-Minute e-Learning Case Study:
Reducing Costs to 30% and Increasing Speed by 300% of Development

Chapter

3-Minute e-Learning Case Study
Reducing Costs to 30% and Increasing Speed by 300% of Development

In this book I have postulated that e-Learning is inherently rapid and has the capability and potential to produce 3-Minute e-Learning formats. Largely, the demand for Rapid e-Learning is born from the dissatisfaction of organizations. They complain that e-Learning is slow, costly and cumbersome to implement. Furthermore, I have argued that e-Learning today has not fulfilled the expectations of creating impact on business performance. Although e-Learning has cut the high cost of training delivery, it has not provided convincing evidence that it contributes to what matters in business – performance!

The big aha! was: We produced a high value program, short and concise, at a faster speed and much lower cost.

To address these issues, I have proposed that we rethink the way we approach e-Learning development by making a shift to 3-Minute e-Learning. Fundamentally, I have stressed that learners are not interested in learning from bloated, boring and time-consuming e-Learning programs. They exhibit e-Learning Behaviors®. They seek out "application points" or performance ideas in all the content they use. Learners have better use for knowledge that provides them with "working proficiency." Their purpose is to apply the ideas instantly in resolving problems and getting results rapidly in their work.

To make the shift from bloated and heavy content to 3-Minute e-Learning, which is light, lean and performance-focused content, I have suggested that we formalize our e-Learning Architecture (e-LA) to conform with the Organic e-Learning Design Principle:

> Learners look for "application points" to apply ideas instantly.
> Invariably, it is also the cheapest and fastest way to rapidly develop
> 3-Minute e-Learning.

Focusing on "application points" allows us the opportunity to cut to the chase. We are able to cut out unnecessary use of time, multimedia, software and complex design that develops the wrong parts of the content. We can apply these resources sparingly on "application points." "Application points" are best displayed in
3-Minute e-Learning formats. By doing so, we provide the learners the focus on

knowledge that boosts "working proficiency."

Case study

To illustrate how to apply 3-Minute e-Learning in the real-world, let me share with you a case study regarding one of our projects. We have repeatedly observed the same outcomes in applying the principles of 3-Minute e-Learning in numerous organizations. Although this case covers a service-oriented company, the lessons learned are applicable to other types of companies and topics.

The problem

The organization we worked with wanted to implement a customer service program for its staff handling in-bound service calls. They had actually begun delivering the program in classroom training as part of the orientation process. The classroom training program took five days. The company was experiencing very high staff turnover in the in-bound sales department. One practical solution to deliver training was to provide an e-Learning solution. Another problem was that the pricing and product information had to be constantly updated and the company felt an e-Learning approach would allow a faster way to update customer support staff on the changes.

Knee-jerk solution

The client organization had decided to convert the existing classroom participant material to an e-Learning format. Since John (the manager) wanted this done rapidly, an in-house Flash developer (Greg) suggested that using Flash would be a logical approach. It would be simple to copy the Word document version of the classroom training materials and display them in Flash. So, in a day, Greg converted a few pages of the content into Flash. The initial result was delivered as a slideshow. Participants could click forward and backward buttons to preview the lessons. John thought that this was not engaging or close to what he envisioned to be a good interactive training. "This will make the staff go to sleep," John said.

It dawned on the team members that it was not effective to simply copy the content from the training manual and turn it into a slide show. They felt the need to develop some interactivity, such as role playing, to help learners identify, for example, the types of complaints from callers. John felt strongly about making this program very interactive and engaging. "Please prepare a plan that is not a knee-jerk solution," John added.

Too slow, too late and not affordable

With help from the instructional designer, writer, graphic artists and voice-over talent, Greg presented a plan. Based on estimates, the Flash program would have these components:

Seven lessons, each with an interactive design:

a. How to greet the caller
b. How to identify the problems of the caller
c. Where to locate answers to caller's questions
d. How to handle the problems
e. How to communicate product changes and pricing
f. How to close the call
g. How to record the incident in the CRM (customer relationship management software)

The interactive design:

a.   Eight role-playing exercises (using Flash, 3 minutes each)

b.   Four interviewing-the-customer games (using Flash, 3 minutes each)

c.   Seven interactive test games (using Flash, 5 minutes each)

d.   Seven narrated slideshows, one for each lesson, an average of 15 pages each, or 90 frames

e.   60 photos and images

John was quite impressed with the plan. However, seeing the costs of $75,000 and 60 days of development, he was certain it was not within his budget and would not meet the 15-day timeline for delivery. Suddenly, panic was in the air.

Prior to this, John and I had met at another company function. John called me to arrange for a meeting. He requested that my team and I explore whether or not this program could be done in 3 weeks for $25, 000. However, he wanted to keep as much interactivity as possible to make the program engaging.

**Fast, cheap - hmmm,
Let's see if we get lucky!**

After the initial meetings with John and his team, these were our findings and discoveries:

1.   Since there was a strong push to get the program delivered quickly, the fastest way was to transfer the classroom hand-out material. "The classroom version has worked for two years and the materials should do

well for e-Learning", John told us.

2. The team depended on the Flash developer for his expertise in multimedia marketing presentations. He was very helpful and easy to work with.

3. The instructional designer was reluctant to go back to the Subject Matter Expert (SME) because the SME already provided the most recent updates on the content. Beside, all of the information required for the training was in the current training manual.

4. Overall, John and the e-Learning team were capable and enthusiastic about the project. The single biggest frustration was that there wasn't enough time and budget to do the job right. They were very receptive and anxious to find ways to deliver the programs faster since it had become a pattern in their company that every internal client wanted e-Learning programs for them done yesterday.

3-Minute e-Learning approach

We requested a half-day session to define the needs and discover solutions. We had two productive brainstorming sessions.

The initial reluctance came from Nancy, the instructional designer. Nancy did not feel comfortable conducting another interview with the SMEs. "We would look foolish and would waste the time of the SME," she said. However, after further review of the SME Discovery Guide (Appendix C), it was the consensus that going back to the SME was not a redundant process, but rather a focused process by asking questions related to application points and organic illustrations. The objective of interviewing the SME was to prioritize, categorize and discover the top 20% performance issues.

The team agreed to review and implement the 3-Minute e-Learning approach. The findings helped them figure out the most pressing issues of the inbound service calls.

Performance logs and audio recordings

After interviewing the SMEs, the team reported that it was relatively easy to ask the SME questions about finding the application points and prioritizing issues on working proficiencies. The SME reviewed with the team the in-bound support record and some recorded audio sessions between the customer and the support staff. "This was very insightful. The logs and interviews made it easy to discover that there are top issues that needed more attention than others," Nancy commented happily.

These were the key findings of our team:

1. The critical problem areas were learning how to find the new product features, how the pricing affects the customers and the consequent adjustments in the invoicing information. Customers needed the information quickly to adjust their pricing and pass the costs to their end buyers. A slow response in this area would increase the loss of customers.

2. It was important to learn how to review the purchasing and ordering patterns of the customer, so that the in-bound service staff could offer the newest updates on the product that could help customers get more profits from the products.

3. Representing the internal client, the head of the customer support staff informed the e-Learning team that these issues heavily did impact performance of the service staff. The skills required and considered critical would be in these areas. "This is the 20% of the skills requirements that create the 80% results," John noted.

4. When we reviewed the outline of the lessons with the internal client and SME, the internal client confirmed that only two topics should be at the top of the lists, while others would just be nice to have. The two lessons were:

    a. How to handle the problems
    b. How to communicate product changes and pricing

Furthermore, these two topic areas were the sources of the most errors, difficulties in learning, and often the most troublesome customer support issues. The SME suggested that presenting case scenarios and ways to resolve these issues would probably be where the training would get the "biggest bang for their buck."

It was also agreed to spend less time developing a full set of training lessons for those lessons not listed in the priority topics. "Participants can learn these topics by going through the CRM software reference help section or learn on the job by coaching and the use of printed job-aids", according to the internal client.

The big aha!

Interviewing the SME was not a difficult process because we prioritized the most important issues. The Internal client was a big help since he provided direction on what mattered in their operations. He actually directed the SME not to be too technical, but more business-focused.

The alternative design was produced for $18,500, down from $75,000, and it was delivered in two weeks.

The new lesson design is shown below.

Seven lessons:

(Each lesson is an interactive design (text instructions, graphics and references).

a. How to greet the caller (text instructions, graphics and references)
b. How to identify the problems of the caller (text instructions, graphics and references)
c. Where to locate answers to caller's questions (text instructions, graphics and references)
d. How to handle the problems (1 slide show and flow chart)
e. How to communicate product changes and pricing (twelve small scenario cases; simple Flash exercises; short case studies presented using graphics, audio recorded playback from actual cases, text and selection of right choices and insights for each scenario).
f. How to close the call (text instructions and references)
g. How to record the incident in the CRM (customer relationship management software) (text instructions and references)

The interactive design

    a.   Twelve role playing exercises (using simple Flash exercises, 2 minutes each)

    b.   One slideshow, narrated, using Flash (3 minutes)

    c.   60 photos and images

    d.   20 HTML pages with reference text from the CRM help guide

It was decided that each scenario and lesson should take about three minutes or less.

The big aha! was:

"We produced a high value program, short and concise, at a faster speed and much lower cost."

Future of
3-Minute e-Learning and
Rapid e-Learning

Chapter 23

Future of 3-Minute e-Learning and Rapid e-Learning

In April 2006, eLearning Guild released the "Future Directions in e-Learning Research Report 2006." In the report, respondents rated Rapid e-Learning top of the list (79% total increase) as an activity, task or practice that will increase in their organizations in the next twelve months.

I am not surprised by the results.

While others think of Rapid e-Learning as a fad or a nice topic for a conference presentation, there is a lot more under the surface. It is my observation that the demand for Rapid e-Learning is a symptom of a deeper problem in our application of e-Learning. Essentially, many of us keep putting all our energies in finding newer and faster technologies so we can mass produce our training delivery through e-Learning. We focus on "rapid development", and not "rapid learning and application."

3-Minute e-Learning is about rapid learning and application. To help learners leverage technologies, there is a need for us to rethink how we organize, collect, and distribute our content or body of knowledge. Today, technologies such as Web 2.0 and e-Learning 2.0, have so many capabilities to offer. And yet, without the needed change in the way we design content, these technologies will have low or marginal impact on performance of workers.

It is my humble opinion that the demands of organizations are not being fully met by most e-Learning designs and implementations. On one hand, it is agreed that
e-Learning provides major cost-cutting and savings. For many, the savings in travel and unproductive expenses are strong values and are sufficient justification to continue investing in e-Learning. On the other hand, this is only one area where e-Learning is expected to contribute. Many organizations expect that e-Learning: (1) focus on the learner's specific need, (2) provide him or her the briefest period and easiest way to acquire the specific knowledge and skill, (3) to enable the learner's rapid application on-job, and (4) produce performance that achieves the desired business results in the fastest time possible.

Cost reduction will continue to work up to a certain point. The challenge for

many of us in e-Learning is how to help learners perform with more dramatic impact in addition to the cost savings it now provides organizations. The true promise of
e-Learning is creating exponential growth in performance and raising the quality of life and personal satisfaction for the learner. At the end of every business day, e-Learning is evaluated on the economy of cost and the economy of time. This is where the 3-Minute e-Learning and Rapid e-Learning come in as timely, relevant, realistic, and practical solutions.

As I conclude this book, let me share with you what I see in the horizon. I see many exciting possibilities, with the accompanying troublesome challenges. All my observations and propositions below are keyed on 3-Minute e-Learning and Rapid e-Learning. Many of the ideas below echo what other experts project will happen in e-Learning.

1. *Growing love for speed, rapid solutions*

   Our business and organizational cultures have been in love with speed for a long time now. Rapid e-Learning is only one area where we want more speed; organizations' appetite for faster, better and cheaper solutions will continue. We better brace ourselves for this. There will be more demand on trainers for 3-Minute e-Learning, rapid training and e-Learning as commercial and non-profit organizations push to redefine and renew their practices to survive and compete in the digital world.

2. *Dynamic and Real-Time Instructional Systems Design and Rapid ADDIE – Next Generation of ISD*

   The training industry has to reinvent itself. Traditional ISD models are now considered obsolete as ways to develop e-Learning programs. There is a need to adapt or invent solutions that will help e-Learning implementors deliver programs based on 1) up-to-the-minute and current demands of the organization, 2) rapid development of on-demand-as-needed-content, which can be addressed by our 3-Minute e-Learning approach, and 3) an on-going dynamic feedback of what works and what does not work in the programs. We can no longer afford the paper-based, tedious training needs analysis and development of programs, all of which actually take months to complete.

I am pleased to share the news that I have the opportunity to collaborate with some clients to develop this new model. I will report to you about our progress.

3. *Instantaneous ways of measuring training outcomes*

For the past ten years, e-Learning implementation has focused on content delivery. We have not touched the issues of measuring performance contributions and returns on the rapid and fast working conditions. The paper-based methods and assumptions of traditional- training ROI studies are inadequate to gauge learning and performance application especially in e-Learning environments.

Wouldn't it be great to know how learners apply learning ideas before, during and after training. And wouldn't it be valuable to be able to collect immediately (as it happens) data on the actual dollar contributions in sales, cost savings, reduction in inefficiencies or savings from complying with court sanctions and legal requirements? Vignettes for Training, Inc. is releasing an online service called TrainingPayback®. Visit www.TrainingPayback.com. I will report to you our progress on this in future publications.

4. *Performance-focused and "application point" content development – new quality standards*

Many of our skills in content development and writing for e-Learning rely on our formal training from the technical writing school of thought. We are trained to be formalistic, and write with an impersonal tone. This is even truer for SMEs who have technical expertise on their topic areas.

In the years to come, we will see a growth and change in the writing style of content for e-Learning and other e-Learning media. The skills and craft required to produce application points and organics, i.e. stories, anecdotes, cases, scenarios and other ways to engage online learners, will be in demand. New skills and methods will also be needed to isolate from the massive data of ever-increasing content the key critical performance-driven and application point content. Learning to identify and write about the key critical content or application points is going to be valuable for trainers and writers.

5. Critical thinking for online learners

One thing will happen in the workplace for sure : we will bombard our employees with massive data and content as the pace of business change and speed of competition increase. One skill online learners will need is critical thinking. This covers how to evaluate massive data or e-Learning content and, then, decide what content must be learned by employees to enable them to perform their tasks - particularly key performance areas. Learner will need to learn how to identify "application points" and 3-Minute e-Learning opportunities. Furthermore, critical thinking covers learning how to navigate the increasing and ever-changing nature of information and content.

Today, we throw our online learners to e-Learning without helping them develop the skill of thinking critically and knowing how to apply what is valuable. The consequence is that we see more online learners who act like they are sitting in the classroom and listening to a lecture. They wait to be spoon-fed.

The younger generation of learners, who are used to video games, multi-tasking and instant messaging, may have better skills in discovery, critical thinking, judgment and decision-making. Now, if only we could train them to apply their skills to improve performance on the job.

6. Learner-driven, informal and personalized learning

Jay Cross (www.jaycross.com), one of the pioneers in e-Learning, tells us that most of the learning that works is informal learning. I agree with Jay. However, I observe that there are very few learning management systems or knowledge dissemination tools that support informal learning. In the near future, we will see LMSs expanding their capabilities to allow learners to set their own learning paths. Steered away from the usual delivery mode of available
e-Learning programs, learners will be able to use their learning systems to select, schedule and record all types of personal-preference learning. Personal-preference learning may cover all self-directed and informal learning including readings, projects, field trips, peer-to-peer collaboration and learning, videos, audio tapes, conferences, seminars and other types of learning

that may continue to emerge. The function of the LMS is to help learners in organizing, recording and reporting all types of personal and informal learning. This way, organizations encourage self-learning. Organizations can then track, support and reward personal development efforts and informal learning.

7. *Convergence: Mobile technology and social networking and learning*

As I mentioned in the Introductory chapter, recently articles and books discuss about the second Internet boom, referring to the new ways people are living in this knowledge-interactive age. They enjoy the growth opportunities of personal computing, mobility, connectivity, and work productivity like never before. In another article, "Web 2.0," written by Paul Boutin, who contributes to magazines like *Business Week* and *Wired,* he mentions in detail many applications and devices "creating network effects through an 'architecture of participation,' and going beyond the page metaphor or Web 1.0 to deliver rich user experiences."

Who among us has not heard of or actually used Internet services and personal smart machines (i.e. PDAs, smartphones, iPods, etc.) that promote socialization and sharing? Who among us does not recognize that networking sites and software applications such as MySpace.com, LinkedIn, PodCasting, Flicker, Blogs and WIKIs have been shaping how people communicate, socialize, and learn together all at the same time. The lines between all of these activities have blurred, but with positive and effective results nonetheless.

What is the impact of these tools to learning? We will see in the future that training and learning will begin to morph with immediate sharing and application of ideas and knowledge in work problem solving. Because mobile technologies and social machines help us to interact with each other faster, we will be able to focus on applying ideas, rather than learning. As this trend continues, we will need more 3-Minute e-Learning formats for our content.

8. *Third generation of LMS - Turbo-Charged or e-Learning Performance Systems*

In my introduction, I mentioned that Elliott Masie wrote about "18 Wishes for an LMS" (www.masie.com, March 21, 2006). The one I like the most is number 8: "LMS, I want you to be more integrated with our business objectives. As we roll out new products, change our strategy, realign our workforce or add new customers, you need to be hooked into the process in real time." Traditionally, training and learning remotely support business strategies for rapid product roll-outs, instant change in work groups and immediate sharing of knowledge. To bring 3-Minute e-Learning and Rapid e-Learning closer to support business strategies, LMSs must creatively use tools like organizational assessments and customer feedback to inform workers and managers how their performance impacts their customers. For example, in a store, by receiving immediate feedback from customers, and allowing workers and managers to instantly view the feedback, the learning requirements and problem solving in that specific store will be focused. Instead of corporate-sponsored customer surveys which are kept secret to top level executives, feedback will be close to those people who can take immediate action. This is one way an LMS can immediately align content and learning to help learners learn, based on gaps and skills as perceived by customers.

9. *Micro content for micro, 3-Minute e-Learning and Rapid e-Learning*

The focus of 3-Minute e-Learning and Rapid e-Learning is instant delivery of knowledge to help workers and managers apply ideas to solve problems and exploit opportunities. This goal is only achievable if those who develop and produce content deliver micro content and encourage micro learning with application points.

As organizations push for more speed and social and mobile technologies encourage micro content, we will witness a shift from the mindset and practice of developing programs. Bloated and heavy curriculum-based (school-like) driven content does not respond to demands for instant and rapid flow, for just-in-time and just-as-needed, just-enough-for-now of micro-content. SMEs, instructional designers, developers and knowledge experts will risk being irrelevant if they do not change their skill sets.

Where will the pressure come from? From the new learners, new managers and business executives who will not wait for curriculum-based training to happen. They will use what they can to train people immediately – even bypassing or ignoring traditional training departments.

10. e-Learning implementation and human factors will continue to be challenge number one

Many e-Learning implementors overestimate the technology problems and underestimate the human problems in adapting to and implementing e-Learning technologies.

According to Lance Dublin, (www.lancedublin.com) a thought leader in e-Learning implementation, "Some organizations fail to achieve the results they want because they don't adequately prepare for the change that e-Learning represents. Make no mistake about it; implementing e-Learning is tough. It takes planning and preparation, leadership and accountability, communications and education, and support and commitment. It takes effective change management."

My experience has shown me that over 50% of the issues involved in deploying e-Learning embody the politics of implementation. Politics here does not mean only the negative stuff that goes on between leaders or departments. It means that there is a power base that must be convinced and persuaded about e-Learning benefits. Many failures in implementation of e-Learning stem from the failure to differentiate the technical change from the people culture change that must always go together.

To succeed, e-Learning implementors will require more skill to navigate and help leaders and managers guide the transition of their organization's way of learning into technology-assisted forms.

11. Replacing the role of trainers as middlemen or middlewomen

Google or e-Bay have been successful because the system supports the desire of their users to go directly to the source and do what they want: in e-Bay to barter and trade unobstructed by middle merchants; in Google, the ability to access information to meet immediate needs. **In the future we will see these changes happening to the role of trainers**. It has finally dawned on practitioners in HRD and training that, for a long time now, they have been serving as middleware providers. Training has had to be delivered and mediated. Now and in the future, due to demands for 3-Minute e-Learning and the availability of tools and systems, learners would rather learn by themselves to get what they want quickly. Organizations will also like this, because it would reduce the costs of training and increase immediate applications on the jobs.

As an illustration, Joe DiDonato, EVP of Learning Technologies at Countrywide Home Loans, Inc. in his keynote presentation at "The Workforce Performance 2006 Conference" in Las Vegas, last September 11, 2006, spoke of his organization's push to help their employees have faster and better access to knowledge and information so they can use the knowledge immediately. He projects the continuing drop in classroom training, especially in those areas where technology-assisted learning can do a better job. "The role of trainers and instructional designers will evolve into knowledge managers."

The implications are that in the future, organizations that can adjust the roles of trainers to facilitate rapid learning will likely continue to add value, whereas those who cannot will disappear. There is a need to cut this major inefficiency in the training industry. The only way to facilitate rapid learning is not to get in the way – but, rather, allow learners with their tools to seek out how they learn best and apply their knowledge and skills. After all, we as trainers, are really facilitators to help learners learn.

Summary

Chapter 24

Summary

This book has addressed key areas found to be problems in producing content that learners are able to use instantly to do their jobs. It has also addressed the challenges of costly and slow e-Learning development. Four prominent problems we often encounter are: a lack of innovative approaches in instructional design, difficulties working with Subject Matter Experts (SMEs), under-utilization and poor management of software and e-Learning tools and the inability to link e-Learning with performance.

3-Minute e-Learning and Rapid e-Learning is about helping learners learn rapidly. It is about improving our organization's ability to deliver learning experiences using the fastest and cheapest possible ways. There are four cornerstones.

The first key component of 3-Minute e-Learning and Rapid e-Learning is design and implementation of an e-Learning Architecture (e-LA) that meets our business needs. The e-LA makes it possible for us to identify and select the best approach, and helps in replicating a production process that meets rapid development needs, reduces cost, and improves the learning experience.

Without the e-LA, we fall victim to the habit of selecting the software and technology because they are cool or fashionable. We become too technology-driven at the expense of the learning outcomes. We fail to master the production process for rapid development.

The second key component of 3-Minute e-Learning and Rapid e-Learning is content design. There is a need to rethink and restructure our content design in order to rapidly deploy e-Learning programs. With Organic e-Learning Design Process, we can move away from bloated, linear and heavy content (data dump) designs (often remnants of converted classroom training) to delivery of application points, "working proficiency knowledge", performance-specific, lean and "must-have" knowledge and information. This will allow the learner to access the knowledge and apply the skills instantly. Achieving this end result requires a fundamentally new way of thinking through instructional design. With this new

203

way of developing content, we are able to train and orient our SMEs and give them faster ways to provide content.

The third key component of 3-Minute e-Learning and Rapid e-Learning is software implementation, management and reusability. Selecting software and managing an LMS make up a combined asset that trainers and developers must control, share and collaborate on with IT. Carefully matching the software and LMS to meet our needs is critical. We can either underestimate or overestimate our needs. This is also true with selecting software developers and programmers. Reusability is a business decision, more than a trainer or programmer decision. e-Learning project leaders must understand that the need to develop e-Learning more quickly drives requirements for optimizing and reusing authoring tools for tests, lessons, exercises and games. Leaders need to direct software developers to factor reusability into every tool they use.

The last key component of Rapid e-Learning is the implementation of a team collaborative process and set of tools. The main goal is to reduce repetitive paper processes that waste time, energy and resources. Rapid e-Learning becomes easier if team members can leverage collaboration tools like file-sharing, version control, discussion rooms, issues-tracking, streamlined approvals, and project management. The biggest challenge is to manage the transition of training production from paper into more software-driven or systems-driven work processes.

In the chapter on Turbo-LMS and e-Learning Business Performance Metrics, we covered examples and cases on how small content such as 3-Minute e-Learning can add to the viability or facility of adding more capabilities to our LMSs. We can add search, bookmarks, and send email with the web address (URL) of the content. We also explored how 3-Minute e-Learning can be used to conduct Rapid ADDIE. Furthermore, 3-Minute e-Learning allows us the facility to link the small and concise content with specific performance metrics. This enables us to correlate
e-Learning with on-the-job performance.

In conclusion, 3-Minute e-Learning and Rapid e-Learning are, first and foremost, about achieving results for both the organization and the learner. e-Learning technologies are robust and inexpensive. But applying 3-Minute e-Learning and Rapid e-Learning requires a new set of thinking, attitudes and inspired leadership if we are to achieve the desired results. e-Learning has to be rapid-performance driven if we are to realize the benefits.

The eLearning Guild Research

The Rapid e-Learning Development Research Report

In April 2006, eLearning Guild released the "Future Directions in e-Learning Research Report 2006." In the report, respondents rated **Rapid e-Learning** top of the list (79% total increase) as an activity, task or practice that will increase in their organizations in the next twelve months. Visit www.elearningguild.com to access more information.

The report is presented with the permission of eLearning Guild.

THE eLEARNING
GUILD ™
Research

The Rapid e-Learning Development Research Report

ANALYSIS AND COMMENTARY BY JOE PULICHINO

There may be no hotter topic in today's e-Learning business than rapid e-Learning development. As the Guild Research Committee considered this phenomenon, we began to question what was really meant by rapid e-Learning development. Is it simply a slick marketing buzz-word created to sell the latest development tools, or is there really substance to the term? Is there an emerging set of best practices that truly constitute a replicable, scalable design process known as rapid e-Learning development? We do know that e-Learning development cycles can be long and costly, and reducing time and expense in this area seems to be a key driver for organizations who have embraced e-Learning.

In February 2005 the eLearning Guild conducted a poll on the topic of rapid e-Learning. Significantly, 31% of respondents reported that their organizations were focused on "rapid e-Learning," but on the other hand 35% of the poll takers selected the choice: "What is rapid e-Learning?" As a follow-up to this poll, Bill Brandon wrote a Guild Whitepaper, *Exploring the Definition of "Rapid e-Learning,"* which examines the different ways that e-Learning professionals look at this new practice. During the same period the Guild Research Committee published a more comprehensive and extensive survey in attempt to find out what is going on in the community around the practice of rapid e-Learning design. The results of that survey are pre-

sented in this report.

As Diane Archibald points out in her January 2005 article, "Rapid e-Learning: A Growing Trend," in ASTD's *Learning Circuits*, "Traditional development methods involve using subject matter experts (SMEs) to pass on information to the instructional designer who, in turn, designs the solution. A developer then builds the interactive solution based on this design, and the quality assurance team tests the solution against the design and development cycles, which can reduce the effectiveness of material with critical timelines or content that is constantly changing." What Ms. Archibald describes is indeed a time consuming process, and as our survey respondents report, one that is simply too

Page Guide to the Report

Continued from page 1

lengthy to accommodate the organizational demands and business drivers for time-sensitive learning, especially in the cases of increasing the product and technical knowledge of customer-facing employees. Hence the solution we are coming to know as rapid e-Learning design.

While it is too early to come to many definitive conclusions, the results presented in this report indicate that adoption rates of rapid e-Learning design are indeed growing and will likely continue to increase. Yet, there are many factors at play: tools, processes, content types, the role of SMEs, and the increasing importance of quality instructional design. The proper mix to use to get rapid e-Learning design right remains a challenge and opportunity. Nonetheless, there seems to be a strong and pervasive belief that rapid e-Learning design can achieve decreases in time to market for e-Learning projects without sacrificing quality.

This report is the Guild's first study of this topic, and as such sets out a baseline from which we will continue to observe the evolution of this new and promising e-Learning practice.

I especially want to acknowledge Research Committee member Dr. David J. Brand of the 3M Corporation for providing much of the insightful commentary and analysis presented in this report.

Demographics

We asked our respondents to identify themselves and their organizations by five attributes: their role in their organization, the size of their organization, the type of their organization, their organization's primary business focus, and the department they work for. This section presents the demographic data of our survey sample.

This survey, like all other Guild surveys, was open to Guild Members and Associates as well as to occasional web-site visitors. These surveys are completed by accessing the survey link on the homepage of the Guild website. Naturally, Guild Members and Associates are more likely than non-members to participate, because each of the more than 16,000 Members and Associates receive an email notifying them of the survey and inviting them to participate. For this reason, we can classify this survey as a random sample because all members have an opportunity to participate, and their participation is random.

Q1. What is your role in your organization?

32%	Instructional Designer
28%	Management
10%	Executive ("C" Level and VPs)
10%	Course Developer
8%	Instructor, Teacher, or Professor
12%	Other

0% | 10% | 20% | 30% | 40% | 50% | 60% | 70% | 80% | 90% | 100%

The single largest response group was "Instructional Designer" (32%). This survey also drew a significant number of responses from "Management" and "Executive" who together accounted for 38% of the survey sample. Those respondents in the "Course Developer" and "Instructor, Teacher, or Professor" groups had the lowest frequencies at 10% and 8% respectively.

Q2. What is the size of your organization?

26%	Under 100
15%	101 to 500
15%	501 to 2,500
17%	2,501 to 10,000
12%	10,001 to 50,000
15%	50,001 or more

0% | 10% | 20% | 30% | 40% | 50% | 60% | 70% | 80% | 90% | 100%

This survey yielded results similar to those of the previous Guild surveys, however, 56% of survey respondents indicated that they work for organizations with less than 2,501 employees. Over the last 12 Guild surveys this is the highest recorded frequency level for this group as it is normally in the 49% to 51% range. Note that the groups "101 to 500," "501 to 2,500," and "50,001 or more" had almost identical response rates, each accounting for 15%.

Q3. What kind of organization do you work for?

42%	Corporation — Not a learning or e-Learning provider
27%	Corporation — Learning or e-Learning provider
13%	College or University
6%	Government or Military
6%	Individual Consultant
4%	Non-profit Organization
2%	K - 12

0% | 10% | 20% | 30% | 40% | 50% | 60% | 70% | 80% | 90% | 100%

Corporations again led the organization demographic for this survey. Respondents working for corporations accounted for 69% of the survey sample. Corporations are divided into two categories, Non-learning product or service providers, and Learning product or service providers. Between these two categories non-learning provider corporations had the largest response pool and accounted for 42% of all survey responses, or 61% of all corporate respondents. Learning provider corporations comprised approximately 27% of the survey response pool, which is a noticeable increase over the Guild average from the last 12 surveys. Respondents working for colleges or universities made up 13% of the entire survey sample, and is the third largest organization group.

Demographics

Q4. Which of the following best describes your organization's primary business focus?

22%	Commercial Training or Education Services
15%	Financial Services
9%	Technology (Hardware or Software)
7%	Government or Military
7%	Healthcare
5%	Manufacturing
5%	Professional Business Services and Consulting
3%	Non-profit
2%	Retail or Wholesale
2%	Telecommunications
2%	Hospitality, Travel, or Food Service
1%	Transportation or Airlines
1%	Aerospace
1%	Petroleum or Natural Resources
1%	Publishing, Advertising, Media, or PR
1%	Real Estate
1%	Pharmaceuticals or Biosciences
0%	Utilities
0%	Arts and Entertainment
15%	Other

0%   10%   20%   30%   40%   50%   60%   70%   80%   90%   100%

Survey respondents were asked to identify the primary business focus of their organization. The results show that 22% of survey respondents work for organizations in the Commercial Training and Education Services group. This is a good indication of the relevance and importance of this survey topic to that demographic. Survey respondents working in the Financial Services sector accounted for 15% of the survey sample and this is clearly the largest single group with a vertical market focus.

Q5. What department do you work for?

56%	Training or Education
8%	Information Technology
8%	Human Resources
6%	Research and Development
5%	Sales and Marketing
3%	Engineering or Product Development
2%	Customer Service
12%	Other

0%   10%   20%   30%   40%   50%   60%   70%   80%   90%   100%

Approximately 56% of survey respondents stated that they work in the Training or Education department of their organization. The response rate of those working within the IT and HR departments of their organization was significantly lower than those working in Training or Education; nonetheless, they were the second and third largest response groups, each accounting for approximately 8% of the entire survey response pool.

Defining Characteristics and Context

Q6. When you think of rapid e-Learning, which of the following do you consider to be its defining characteristic? (Select only one.)

34%	Rapid development tools
18%	Shortened design process
9%	Templates to accelerate design
7%	Accelerated project management
7%	Content reusability
6%	Shortened programming cycles
6%	More efficient and effective use of SMEs
6%	Templates to accelerate programming
7%	Other

0% 10% 20% 30% 40% 50% 60% 70% 80% 90% 100%

For this question, we asked survey respondents to select only one choice because we wanted to see what the single most common defining characteristic of rapid e-Learning development was. According to survey respondents, "Rapid development tools" (34%) trump "Shortened design process" (18)% by a nearly 2-to-1 margin. It is interesting to see that this characteristic is most frequently associated with rapid e-Learning development, especially when compared to the results of the next question where "Content review and approval" and "Access to subject matter experts" are cited as the two factors that most frequently slow down the development of e-Learning products. In this case the "More efficient and effective use of SME's" might have received a lower score because other choices were deemed to be more significant and only one choice was permitted for this question. Shortening the design process, the use of templates and content reusability are ways to shorten the development cycle, and when you group all three together they make up a significant 31%. Therefore, while many respondents view rapid e-Learning through the tools that are used, just as many see the importance of process as a factor in setting the speed of the development.

Q7. Historically, in your organization, which of the following have had the most impact on SLOWING DOWN the development of e-Learning products? (Select up to three choices.)

60%	Content review and approval
53%	Access to subject matter experts
48%	Internal resources available for development of e-Learning
28%	Level of interactivity required
20%	Technology problems
10%	Other
10%	Testing and assessment requirements
2%	Does not apply
0%	I do not know

0% 10% 20% 30% 40% 50% 60% 70% 80% 90% 100%

So, if the development of e-Learning is not fast enough, what slows it down? For this question, we limited respondents to only three choices. Two of the top three reasons suggested for slowing down development are related to content. The high frequency of "Content review and approval" (60%) and "Access to SME's" (53%) show that it is not always the development process itself that lengthens cycle time. It is also obtaining consensus along the way and getting the needed content that can slow things down. Another significant reason cited here is the lack of internal resources. Is this related to size of the organization? Is it related to increased trends in outsourcing? Does this answer indicate respondents still see a need for some internal resources to develop e-Learning, especially in the context of rapid development needs? It is also interesting to note that "technology problems" do not seem to be much of a factor.

How Rapid is Rapid?

Q8. Currently, how many e-Learning projects does your organization typically produce in a quarter where the project life cycle is measured in weeks (or less)? (Select only one.)

16%	None
46%	1 to 5 projects
16%	6 to 10 projects
5%	11 to 15 projects
10%	16 or more projects
3%	Does not apply
4%	I do not know

0% 10% 20% 30% 40% 50% 60% 70% 80% 90% 100%

Note that 62% of the respondents indicated their organizations do only 1 to 10 e-Learning projects each quarter that would fall into most organization's definition of a rapid e-Learning development cycle. This may be indicating that most organizations are still fairly new to this type of development process. It will be interesting to see how this number might increase in the next 6 to 12 months.

Q9. Based on the typical size or complexity of the e-Learning courses your organization produces, which of the following ranges in development time means "rapid e-Learning development" in your organization? (Select only one.)

6%	1 week or less
17%	1 to 2 weeks
28%	2 to 4 weeks
24%	4 to 8 weeks
13%	8 to 12 weeks
3%	More than 12 weeks
6%	Does not apply
3%	I do not know

0% 10% 20% 30% 40% 50% 60% 70% 80% 90% 100%

Note that the majority of respondents (52%) indicated that a typical rapid e-Learning development cycle for their organization falls in a 2 to 8 week time frame. It would be interesting to compare this time frame to more traditional e-Learning development projects in their organizations and to see what percentage decrease in development length is achieved when a "rapid" approach is used.

Organizational Demand

Q10. Is your organization demanding more rapid development and deployment of e-Learning courses, projects, and initiatives? (Select only one.)

38% Yes, significant demand

40% Yes, moderate demand

14% No, not to any noticeable degree

4% No, not at all

3% Does not apply

1% I do not know

0% | 10% | 20% | 30% | 40% | 50% | 60% | 70% | 80% | 90% | 100%

Note that 78% of survey respondents indicate a moderate to a significant demand when it comes to rapid development and deployment of e-Learning courses. Is this a reflection that developing at the speed of business is the critical driver as compared to the speed of instructional design being the constraining factor?

Q11. Is your organization demanding lower costs for development and deployment of e-Learning courses, projects, and initiatives? (Select only one.)

38% Yes, significant demand

32% Yes, moderate demand

18% No, not to any noticeable degree

5% No, not at all

4% Does not apply

3% I do not know

0% | 10% | 20% | 30% | 40% | 50% | 60% | 70% | 80% | 90% | 100%

Clearly, the pressure is on to lower costs. Note that a significant majority (70%) reported that their organizations are demanding lower costs. When the "Does not apply" and "I do not know" responses are factored out, the frequency of "Yes" responses reaches 75%. This closely parallels the numbers for these two categories in the previous question, which suggests that people see a correlation between rapid e-Learning and reduced cost. Possibly this is based on the axiom that "time is money."

Trends in Adoption

Q12. Is your organization formally engaged in the practice of rapid e-Learning development and deployment of e-Learning courses, projects, and initiatives? (Select only one.)

27% Yes, on a regular and consistent basis for most projects

25% Yes, but only for selected or special projects

20% Yes, but only on an experimental or beginner's level

15% No, but we are planning to do so in 2005

8% No, and we have no plans to

2% Does not apply

3% I do not know

0%   10%   20%   30%   40%   50%   60%   70%   80%   90%   100%

Here the majority of respondents (72%) indicated they are currently involved in rapid e-Learning projects. Another 15% see themselves as entering into this arena in the next year. So the vast majority of organizations see themselves as having learning needs and delivery requirements that fit into a rapid e-Learning development framework. These results are probably the best indicator we have that rapid e-Learning development is not so much hype as it is an emerging best practice.

Q13. Regarding the number of e-Learning products to be developed using a rapid methodology in 2005, which of the following best describes your organization's direction? (Select only one.)

21% Dramatic increase in rapid e-Learning development

33% Moderate increase in rapid e-Learning development

23% Slight increase in rapid e-Learning development

11% No change in level of rapid e-Learning development

1% Decrease in rapid e-Learning development

6% No rapid e-Learning development

5% I do not know

0%   10%   20%   30%   40%   50%   60%   70%   80%   90%   100%

Note that 77% of the survey respondents see at least some level of increase in the practice of rapid e-Learning development in 2005. This suggests there is time-critical information that needs to be made available to the target audiences for the e-Learning. One striking element of the responses to these questions is the small percentage of the "I do not know" answers (5%). This suggests that this is a mainstream area of consideration for most organizations represented by the respondents to this survey.

Business Drivers

Q14. What is the primary reason driving your organization to rapid development and deployment of e-Learning courses, projects, and initiatives? (Select only one.)

%	
32%	Short time-to-market requirement due to project cycle time
14%	Lack of development resources to meet deadlines
11%	Short time-to-market requirement due to poor planning
11%	Dependencies on factors over which there is little control
9%	Workload increase which is either unexpected or cyclical
11%	Other
8%	Does not apply
4%	I do not know

0% 10% 20% 30% 40% 50% 60% 70% 80% 90% 100%

The most frequently cited driver for the use of rapid e-Learning methodology is shorter time-to-market. The need for developing at the speed of business is evident. Lack of development resources and poor planning on some past projects are also driving organizations to come up with ways to do rapid e-Learning. Apparently the hope and the promise here is to circumvent some of the barriers that have slowed down the development of e-Learning in the past. We were expecting poor planning and project management to be more of a factor, but it seems that this is not really much of an issue in most respondents' organizations.

Q15. In your organization, what content areas are most likely to derive the greatest benefit from a rapid e-Learning development process: (Select all that apply.)

%	
56%	Product training for employees, partners, and customers
53%	Technology training for employees, partners, and customers
29%	Regulatory compliance
28%	Organizational change initiatives
25%	Business and management skills
24%	Customer service
23%	Sales productivity
18%	Call center productivity
11%	Other
6%	I do not know

0% 10% 20% 30% 40% 50% 60% 70% 80% 90% 100%

Product training (56%) and technology training (53%) are by far the most frequently cited content areas where the greatest benefit can be realized through the practice of rapid e-Learning development. This should not be surprising as the need in these content areas is based on the importance of the timeliness of this information, and the fact that this information may change often so that it may need to be modified or updated frequently and quickly. Clearly, this points out that there are contexts in which rapid e-Learning development is more critical to project success than in others. If this is true, however, we wonder why sales productivity showed up so much lower on the scale.

Keys and Methods

Q16. In your opinion, what are the three keys to rapid instructional design for e-Learning content? (Select only three.)

%	Key
77%	Infrastructure to support rapid design (technology, etc.)
60%	Innovation in instructional design strategies
40%	Improved content management and use of LCMSs
40%	Concurrent phases of instructional design process
23%	Reduction of some phases of instructional design process
15%	Working faster
9%	Outsourcing of some phases of instructional design process
8%	Other
2%	I do not know

0% 10% 20% 30% 40% 50% 60% 70% 80% 90% 100%

For this question we asked respondents to select the three most important keys to rapid e-Learning design. The clear leader is "Infrastructure to support rapid design" (77%). Certainly, a process can move no more quickly than its slowest point, so to enable a rapid process we need to have a complete infrastructure that can help speed the process up, such as available templates to serve as starting points. The fact that innovation in instructional design strategies also had a high response percentage indicates that traditional instructional design models will either have to be set aside and replaced, or updated to make them more flexible and nimble in light of the "demands" of rapid e-Learning.

Q17. What methods does your organization employ to facilitate rapid design and production of e-Learning content? (Select all that apply.)

%	Method
71%	Design templates
49%	Programming templates
45%	Reusable graphics objects
44%	Content outlines
43%	Storyboard templates used for quick assembly of content
32%	Reusable topics or blocks of content
8%	Other
7%	Does not apply
1%	I do not know

0% 10% 20% 30% 40% 50% 60% 70% 80% 90% 100%

The use of templates (both design and programming) and "reusable" graphic objects to help the process not have to "start from scratch" helps to shorten the development cycle. Content outlines and storyboards also help frame the process, and are designed to help get consensus faster.

Subject Matter Experts

Q18. Which one of the following statements is most often true concerning how Subject Matter Experts (SMEs) in your organization provide content to instructional designers and developers? (Select only one.)

65%	SMEs give us content in any manner and we work with it
14%	SMEs fill out specific design forms which we work with
7%	SMEs input content directly using development tools
3%	SMEs do not provide us with content
6%	Other
3%	Does not apply
2%	I do not know

0% 10% 20% 30% 40% 50% 60% 70% 80% 90% 100%

The majority of respondents indicated they work with the content in whatever way they receive it from the SME. Would having templates that the SME's populate with content shorten the development cycle? On the other hand, would it take the SME's longer to get the content to the designers if they had to use templates? Perhaps it is a mixture of both.

Q19. What tools do you employ with Subject Matter Experts (SMEs) to help you develop e-Learning content? (Select all that apply.)

70%	Interviews
42%	Standardized Word or Excel templates to gather information
30%	Email questionnaires or surveys
25%	Specific content-structured questionnaires
23%	Focus groups
11%	Other
7%	Does not apply

0% 10% 20% 30% 40% 50% 60% 70% 80% 90% 100%

An interview process (70%) is the most common method for engaging SME's to help in the content development process. Questionnaires using standardized templates (42%) is a much less frequently used method. In some respects this is one of the more labor intensive and important areas in the development cycle, because if the content is flawed the final product is likely to have little value. Clearly, this is an area where we can have a classic trade-off between speed and quality. It is possible that some of the greatest innovations in rapid e-Learning practice will come in the area of getting content from SMEs faster without compromising the quality of the content.

Outsourcing

Q20. Does your organization outsource or out-task some or all of e-Learning projects that need a quick turn-around? (Select only one.)

8%	All the time
30%	Only when necessary
26%	Rarely
27%	Never
6%	Does not apply
3%	I do not know

0% 10% 20% 30% 40% 50% 60% 70% 80% 90% 100%

According to our survey respondents 53% report that outsourcing is not an option for achieving rapid e-Learning development. Does this mean that outsourcing, while having the benefit of increasing available resource, does not have the benefit of increasing speed of development? Perhaps for e-Learning development to be rapid it must be done in-house where infrastructure can be controlled and managed, and SMEs can be more easily and quickly accessed.

Content Sources

Q21. In your organization, where does the content for e-Learning courses and products typically come from? (Select all that apply.)

%	
86%	Subject Matter Experts (SMEs)
67%	Internally developed by instructional designers and developers
65%	Classroom materials
55%	Technical documentation
37%	Company literature
25%	Collateral marketing material and documents
17%	Externally developed custom content
13%	Externally developed off-the-shelf content
4%	Other
0%	Does not apply
0%	I do not know

0% 10% 20% 30% 40% 50% 60% 70% 80% 90% 100%

"SME's" (86%) are cited as the number one source of content information. Is this because they hold much tacit information that needs to be made explicit and e-Learning is one of the ways of making this information available to a wider audience? Pre-existing "Classroom materials" (65%) and "Technical documentation" (55%) are also key sources, but in many situations where the information is already available, it may not be quite so scalable when it comes to sharing it with a wider audience.

Q22. What are the most common types of content and documents that your organization uses to develop e-Learning content? (Select all that apply.)

%	
74%	PowerPoint slides
70%	Word documents
50%	Manuals
49%	PDFs
42%	Flash files
23%	Hand-written notes
14%	Other

0% 10% 20% 30% 40% 50% 60% 70% 80% 90% 100%

"PowerPoint slides" (74%) are the number one source, and "Word documents" (70%) are a close second as the most common types of content documents used in e-Learning. This is not surprising, however disappointing it may be to both instructional designers and learners. But then again, these are fairly ubiquitous tools that most SME's are familiar with. "PDFs" (49%) allow for a broader range of sources of the content and possibly do a better job of preserving the look and feel of the original content that can come from a variety of sources. It will be interesting to see how tools such as Articulate and Captivate that animate PowerPoint will influence rapid e-Learning development.

Cost

Q23. In terms of cost per instructional hour, which of the following best describes the cost of rapid e-Learning development methodology, relative to traditional methods of development for your organization? (Select only one.)

2%	Rapid methods cost significantly more
6%	Rapid methods cost slightly more
12%	Rapid methods cost about the same
23%	Rapid methods cost slightly less
28%	Rapid methods cost significantly less
29%	I do not know

0% 10% 20% 30% 40% 50% 60% 70% 80% 90% 100%

The majority of respondents (63%) indicated that rapid methods of development cost the same as or less than traditional methods of development. This would appear to be good news as expense should therefore not be a barrier to taking up the practice of rapid e-Learning development. In fact, it may become a selling point for its adoption.

Staffing Requirements for Success

Q24. In terms of staffing your organization to be successful on projects requiring a rapid development framework, which skill sets are most critical? (Select up to three choices.)

81%	Instructional design
46%	Project management
43%	Subject matter expertise
24%	Graphical design
22%	Programming
21%	Technical knowledge of infrastructure requirements
14%	Technical writing
11%	Web design
5%	Other
4%	Meta-tagging
3%	I do not know

0% 10% 20% 30% 40% 50% 60% 70% 80% 90% 100%

One of the concerns with rapid e-Learning is that in order to achieve a shorter timeline you have to give up something (e.g. interactivity, look and feel, etc.). Perhaps this is why "Instructional design" (81%) received the highest score by far. In order to make rapid e-Learning as effective as possible a professional instructional designer is needed so that quality is not unduly compromised. Just so, "Project management" so that the fast process stays on track also seems critical to many respondents (46%).

Issues of Quality

Q25. **In your opinion, does producing e-Learning rapidly increase or decrease product quality in terms of look and feel and interactivity? (Select only one.)**

9% Increases quality significantly
11% Increases quality moderately
36% Neither increases nor decreases quality
28% Decreases quality moderately
8% Decreases quality significantly
8% I do not know

0% | 10% | 20% | 30% | 40% | 50% | 60% | 70% | 80% | 90% | 100%

More survey respondents (36%) anticipate at least some decrease in quality as a result of using rapid e-Learning methods as compared to those (20%) who think there will be an increase in quality. Is it likely that the perception is that in order to gain something (speed) you have to give up something (quality)? But perhaps, if you do the development of the e-Learning in a different way as compared to the traditional way, and have greater standardization (e.g. quality templates) you can gain more in speed, but have less reduction of quality.

Q26. **In your opinion, does producing e-Learning rapidly change product quality in terms of learner retention and demonstrable changes in learner behavior? (Select only one.)**

6% Increases quality significantly
13% Increases quality moderately
45% Neither increases nor decreases quality
15% Decreases quality moderately
5% Decreases quality significantly
16% I do not know

0% | 10% | 20% | 30% | 40% | 50% | 60% | 70% | 80% | 90% | 100%

About the same percentage of survey respondents see an increase in quality in terms of learner retention (19%) as compared to those who see a decrease in quality (20%) when rapid e-Learning development methods are used. This distribution could be a function of the fact that we are still too new in this area to have significant experience and reliable data to make an accurate determination. At this point, most of what we know about rapid e-Learning design seems to opinions and conjectures, but at least we have a base line to work from as we determine what will work and what best practices will emerge.

Hot Links and Other Resources

Rapid e-Learning: A Growing Trend, by Dianne Archibald
A brief overview of rapid development, and the processes involved from conception to implementation.
http://www.learningcircuits.org/2005/jan2005/archibald.htm

Exploring the Definition of "Rapid e-Learning," by Bill Brandon
An e-Learning Guild white paper on the definition of Rapid e-Learning.
http://www.elearningguild.com/pdf/4/rapid_elearning_whitepaper_3-2-05.pdf

Why Rapid e-Learning is Needed, Altus Learning Systems
A page highlighting Rapid e-Learning and how it fits into training programs.
http://www.altuscorp.com/?m=rapid-elearning&s=2

To learn more about this subjects:

To learn more about this subject, we encourage you to search the following pages on the Guild's Web site using the words "rapid e-Learning design."

The Resource Directory: http://www.eLearningGuild.com/resources/resources/index.cfm?actions=viewcats

The eLearning Developers' Journal: http://www.eLearningGuild.com/articles/abstracts/index.cfm?action=view

*This survey generated responses from over 410 Members and Associates; these results are statistically significant and can be generalized to the entire Guild membership.

About the author

Joe Pulichino, Director of Research, The eLearning Guild

Joe Pulichino began his career in education as an English instructor at Rutgers University over 25 years ago. Since then he has held a number of senior management positions in the technology sector where he was responsible for the development, delivery, and marketing of a wide range of corporate education programs and services. Most recently he has served as vice-president of education services at Sybase, vice-president of eLearning at Global Knowledge Network, and CEO of Edu-Point. He is an adjunct faculty member of the Pepperdine University Graduate School of Education and Psychology where he is completing his Ed.D. in Education Technology. The focus of his research is on informal and organizational learning. Joe is principal of the Athena Learning Group, a virtual network of consultants and academics working in the fields of learning, Knowledge Management, performance enhancement and Communities of Practice.

The Research Committee Members

Ms. Dawn Adams, Content Manager, Microsoft Global e-Learning Services

Ms. Karen Allnutt, Instructional Designer and Software Trainer, Steelman Services LLC

Dr. David J. Brand, Learning Design & Technology, 3M Corporation

Ms. Paula Cancro, IT Training Specialist, IFMG, Inc.

Mr. Jerry Day, Sr. Technical Training Developer, Pillar Data Systems

Ms. Barbara Fillicaro, Writer, Training Media Review

Ms. Silke Fleischer, Product Manger, Macromedia

Dr. Silvia R. Folts, President, Distance Instruction

Mr. Joe Ganci, CEO, Dazzle Technologies, Corp.

Dr. Nancy Grey, Director, Pharmaceutical Regulatory Education, Pfizer

Ms. Sheila Jagannathan, e-Learning Specialist, The World Bank Institute

Dr. Warren Longmire, Manager, Learning Strategy, Convergys

Dr. Maggie Martinez, CEO, The Training Place

Mr. Frank Nyguen, Senior Learning Technologist, Intel

Mr. Eric Rosen, Online Learning Strategist, Stanford University

Dr. Patti Shank, Managing Partner, LearningPeaks, LLC

Dr. Richard Smith, Instructional Designer, Amerind

Ms. Celisa Steele, Chief Creative Officer, Isoph

Mr. Ernie Thor, Senior Instructional Designer, Cingular Wireless

Ms. Angela van Barneveld, Sr. Learning Design Specialist, Canada Customs and Revenue Agency

About the Guild

The eLearning Guild is a global Community of Practice for designers, developers, and managers of e-Learning. Through this member-driven community, the *Guild* provides high-quality learning opportunities, networking services, resources, and publications.

Guild members represent a diverse group of instructional designers, content developers, Web developers, project managers, contractors, consultants, managers and directors of training and learning services – all of whom share a common interest in e-Learning design, development, and management. Members work for organizations in the corporate, government, academic, and K-12 sectors. They also are employees of e-Learning product and service providers, consultants, students, and self-employed professionals.

The more than 16,000 plus members of this growing, worldwide community look to the *Guild* for timely, relevant, and objective information about e-Learning to increase their knowledge, improve their professional skills, and expand their personal networks.

The eLearning Developers' Journal is the premier weekly online publication of *The eLearning Guild*. The Journal showcases practical strategies and techniques for designers, developers, and managers of e-Learning.

The eLearning Guild organizes a variety of industry events focused on participant learning:

Online Events...	The eLearning Guild's **ONLINE FORUM.** SERIES Thursdays	THE LMS/LCMS IMPLEMENTATION & MANAGEMENT ONLINE SYMPOSIUM July 27-29, 2005	THE ELEARNING MANAGEMENT ONLINE SYMPOSIUM October 5-7, 2005	THE RAPID ELEARNING DEVELOPMENT ONLINE SYMPOSIUM April 27-29, 2005
Face-to-face Events...	eLearning **Producer.** CONFERENCE & EXPO 2005 March 14-17, 2005	INSTRUCTIONAL DESIGN CONFERENCE June 20-24, 2005	DEVLEARN. THE ELEARNING DEVELOPERS' CONFERENCE & EXPO 2005 November 15-18, 2005	

3-Minute e-Learning
Organic e-Learning Design Process®
Ray E. Jimenez, Ph.D.

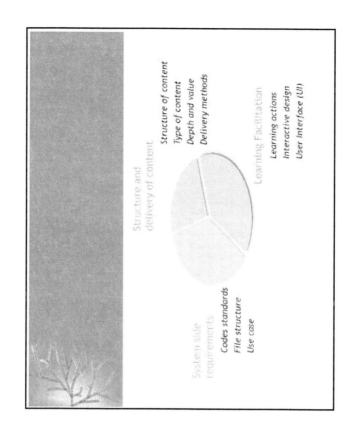

System side requirements
Codes standards
File structure
Use case

Structure and delivery of content
Structure of content
Type of content
Depth and value
Delivery methods

Learning Facilitation
Learning actions
Interactive design
User interface (UI)

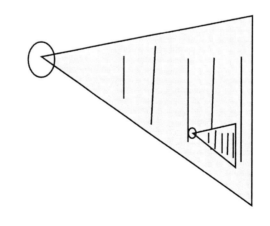

Appendix B

3-Minute e-Learning   *Organic e-Learning Design* ®

Table of Contents

3-Minute e-Learning and Organic e-Learning Design Process

Online Illustrations, Demos, and Examples

Please access the secure site to preview the demos and examples illustrated in this book.

This web site is constantly being updated.

www.vignettestraining.com

1. Complete the request form to obtain your login information.

2. If you need more assistance or you wish to contact Ray Jimenez, please send an email to rjimenez@vignettestraining.com

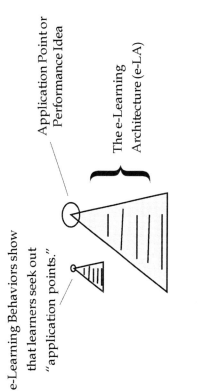

e-Learning Behaviors show that learners seek out "application points."

Application Point or Performance Idea

The e-Learning Architecture (e-LA)

3-Minute e-Learning
Organic e-Learning Design Process
By Ray E. Jimenez, Ph.D.

Overriding Principle

The key principle that guides the Organic e-Learning Design Process is this: "Learners look for **application points** to apply ideas instantly. Invariably, it is also the cheapest and fastest way to rapidly develop e-Learning programs."

The Organic e-Learning Design Process provides the detailed step-by-step procedure to accomplish the principle. 3-Minute e-Learning is the outcome.

Purpose

Organic e-Learning Design helps you in:

1. Understanding the principles and concepts to guide e-Learning course design and development that meets the learner's and the organization's needs.

2. Implementing the mechanics and procedures covered in the course design and development.

3. Learning how to use the design process as the basis for developing 3-Minute e-Learning and e-Learning Architecture (e-LA) and determining systems and software requirements of the project.

4. Learning the skills and mind-set required to produce sound e-Learning courses.

5. Producing a budget, timeline and documentation that you can provide to developers or vendors.

The e-Learning Implementation Process

The flow chart below covers the total e-Learning implementation process.
Organic e-Learning Design Process pertains to the development of
3-Minute e-Learning snippets, nuggets, chunks and vignettes.

3-Minute e-Learning   *Organic e-Learning Design*®

The Common Pitfalls In e-Learning Course Development

The flow chart below covers the total e-Learning implementation process. **Organic e-Learning Design** pertains to the development of **3-Minute e-Learning** snippets, nuggets, chunks and vignettes.

1. Migrating to e-Learning those courses designed for classroom training or print delivery.

2. Purchasing software before defining the e-Learning course design.

3. Designing and developing e-Learning programs without understanding the principles of **e-Learning Behaviors** and the nature of Internet technologies.

4. Adapting traditional instructional design in e-Learning course development without critical thought.

5. Fatal mistake

Developing an e-Learning program to fit specific software without going through the design process. It's costly and presents constraints in realizing the full benefits of e-Learning.

---

e-Learning Project Development Flow

Readiness Study
Viability Study
Learning Strategies

ROI/Planning/Justifications
RFQs

e-Learning Architecture
Learning Objectives
Design Process
Storyboarding
User Interface
Interactivity
Multimedia

Requirements
Features and Functions
Selecting Software
LMS -Learning
Mgmt Systems

Software & Systems

Course
Development
3-Minute e-Learning

Prototyping
Testing
Infrastructure
Hosting
Coding

Web

Software

Database
Servers

Piecing
Together

Avoiding the Common Pitfalls In e-Learning Course Development

There is a need to clearly understand that before applying a software solution, these three conditions must be met:

a. An instructional thought process or design is undertaken.

b. The instructional thought or design is documented and communicated.

c. A plan is developed with costing and timelines based on the instructional thought or design.

It is only with the above information that you would have a clear idea of what and how to transform the content into 3-Minute e-Learning.

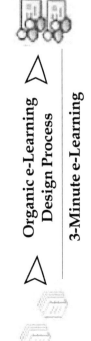

Organic e-Learning Design Process

3-Minute e-Learning

The purpose of Appendix B is to provide a step-by-step guide in achieving these three preconditions.

3-Minute e-Learning *Organic e-Learning Design*®

5-Step Development Process

There are five essential steps to prepare a sound design for 3-Minute e-Learning programs. The process starts with analysis of content and ends in developing technical specifications for each lesson page.

Steps 1 and 2 fall under
Organic Design Decisions

Steps 3, 4 and 5 fall under
Organic Production Process

1 **Analyzing and Categorizing
Content**

2 **Developing Lesson Pages**

3 **Developing Interface and
Interactive Design**

4 **Selecting the Methods
and Tools**

5 **Preparing Budgets and Documentation
for Lesson Pages**

3-Minute e-Learning   *Organic e-Learning Design*®

5-Step Development Process

These are the details of each step.

Steps 1 and 2 fall under
Organic Design Decisions

Steps 3, 4 and 5 fall under
Organic Production Process

1

Analyzing and Categorizing Content

Breaking down content into organized and relevant parts and pieces. This categorization helps trainers lay out content on lesson pages to enable learners to have better control of the learning process.

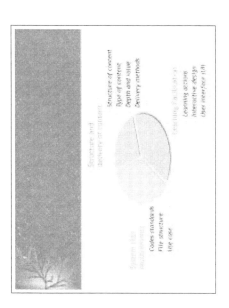

2

Developing Lesson Pages

The content is laid out on the appropriate type of pages with relationship of thought and content carefully considered to ensure that learning starts with "must learn" topics and then moves to "in-depth and detailed" content. Covered here are: **Laying out pages, and writing and designing e-Learning programs.**

3

Developing Interface and Interactive Design

The content and the pages are tested and converted into a schematic that guides in the development of navigation, flow and relationships of the different elements.

4

Selecting The Methods and Tools

This process allows trainers to evaluate and assess the types of tools and methods they wish to employ to achieve the program goals.

5

Preparing Budgets and Documentation for Lesson Pages

This final step helps trainers and developers convey their design into documentation that contains the features, functions and systems requirements as well as costing and timing. This step bridges the e-Learning process to software selection and development process.

3-Minute e-Learning *Organic e-Learning Design*®

Step 1 - Analyzing and Categorizing Content

To prepare, write, edit, convert, modify or adjust content for e-Learning, follow the 5-Step Development Process. The design process should be guided by the results of the readiness and viability studies and e-Learning strategy decisions.

This approach in developing e-Learning programs is based on the discoveries about how learners learn, how they find and apply "application points", and **e-Learning Behaviors.**

NOTE:
A lesson is a unit of knowledge that contains an understandable body of information. A lesson may be delivered in 3-Minute e-Learning. Before you start with (A), break down your program into an outline with modules and lessons. Lessons contain small or granular ideas, snippets or vignettes of your content. Once you have identified a lesson, proceed with (A).

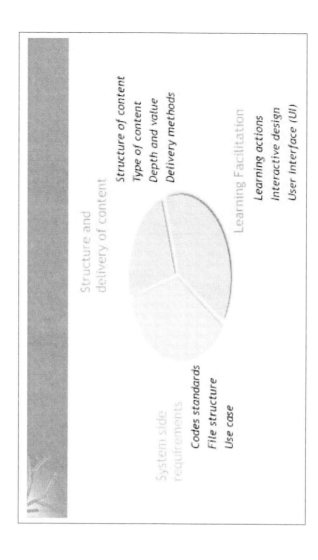

A **Structure of Content**

B **Analysis of Content**

C **Nature of Content**

3-Minute e-Learning   *Organic e-Learning Design*®

Step 1 - Analyzing and Categorizing Content

A ## Structure of Content

Categorize modules and lesson content into 3-Minute e-Learning:

1. Performance outcomes, principles, key ideas ("application points")
2. Processes, tasks, steps, procedures
3. Tools, references, forms
4. People relationships and coordination

You will observe that a typical program consists of approximately 10-20% content that is type (1), while 80% of the content falls in types (2), (3), and (4).

In 3-Minute e-Learning and Organic e-Learning Design, the focus is on performance outcomes. Focusing the e-Learning development on the 20% content reduces the "bloat" and costs of production. It also speeds up development.

The benefits

What benefits can be gained from discovering the structure of your content and focusing on performance content?

1. It allows you to prioritize content and training activities that have higher impact on performance or results.

2. It helps learners focus quickly on learning that truly matters for their respective jobs.

3. It allows you to save time and money. You can allocate the right e-Learning media, tools and solutions to match the type of content.

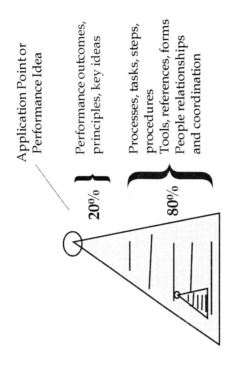

Application Point or Performance Idea

20% — Performance outcomes, principles, key ideas

80% — Processes, tasks, steps, procedures
Tools, references, forms
People relationships and coordination

The only way to identify "application points" is to understand the Structure of Content.

"Application Points" Pyramid

Appendix B

A **Structure of Content - Exercise # 1A**
Macro view of content

Purpose: This exercise helps you identify the categories of content from a macro view. The table of contents provides us a clue of the categories of content.

Activity: Write down in the space provided which item in the table of contents would fall under what category.

Presented below is an example of the structure of content. (This is a fictitious table of contents of a program).

A program wants to train bank tellers what to do in the event of a robbery.

These are some of the contents of the program:

1. How to prepare an accident/incident report.

2. How to stay calm.

3. How to assess and identify potential hold-uppers.

4. How to call the police.

5. How to trigger the alarm.

6. How to help customers stay calm.

7. How to use the reference guide to report the incident.

8. How to understand the laws on company liabilities in case customers are hurt.

9. What the bank insurance covers in this type of incident.

10. How to make sure everyone is safe, including you.

11. Who to call or report to if you notice suspicious persons.

Activity Form

1. Performance outcomes, principles, key ideas ("application points")

_____

_____

2. Processes, tasks, steps, procedures

_____

_____

3. Tools, references, forms

_____

_____

4. People relationships and coordination

_____

_____

A   Structure of Content - Exercise # 1A
Macro view of content

Example of the structure of content
(This is a fictitious table of contents for a program).

A program is needed to train bank tellers what to do in the event of a robbery.

These are some of the contents of the program.

Answers

1. How to prepare an accident/incident report.   `2`

2. How to stay calm.   `1`

3. How to assess and identify potential hold-uppers.   `2`

4. How to call the police.   `2`

5. How to trigger the alarm.   `2`

6. How to help customers stay calm.   `1`

7. How to use the reference guide to report the incident.   `3`

8. How to understand the laws on company liabilities in case customers are hurt.   `3`

9. What the bank insurance covers in this type of incident.   `3`

10. How to make sure everyone is safe, including you.   `1`

11. Who to call or report to if you notice suspicious persons.   `4`

Guide to Content Categories

Here is a guide for categorizing the content.

`1` Performance outcomes, principles, key ideas ("application points")

`2` Processes, tasks, steps, procedures

`3` Tools, references, forms

`4` People relationships and coordination

3-Minute e-Learning   *Organic e-Learning Design*®

A   Structure of Content – Exercise # 1B
3-Minute e-Learning View

Purpose: In Exercise #1A, the illustration of bank teller training, we studied the macro view of the table of contents. In this exercise, #1B, we now study the granular view. By understanding this view, we can further categorize content.

Activity: Study the granular content on the left column and mark which ideas fall into which categories. You may wish to underline and put a corresponding number near the words or phrases in the content to correspond to the categories.

Presented below is an example of the granular content. (This is a fictitious table of contents for a program).

A program is needed to train bank tellers what to do in the event of a robbery.

10. How to make sure everyone is safe, including you. (3-Minute e-Learning). ☐ 1

People react to crisis in different ways. Some may panic at the sign of a threat, whereas others may stay calm and relaxed. In a hold-up situation, there are at least four groups of people: you, co-employees, the robber and your customers. Which person must you manage first? You!

Handling your own emotions is the starting point. How do you handle your emotions? Essentially, learning about your emotions ahead of time is the best way to learn to control them. Your emotions are heavily influenced by the amount of knowledge and information, and your attitudes in a crisis. If your instant reaction is to fight back, you could emotionally charge a crisis situation. You really cannot help others unless you are in control of yourself.

In the guide "How to handle stressful situations," you will find excellent tips on how to be in control. You may also visit the company counselor or view employee assistance programs if you wish to learn more about how you can master stressful situations. The FBI also issued an interesting article on studies of bank hold-ups. This study shows that most often, deaths or loss of life in hold-up situations are low, but there are practical steps to make sure that you avoid fatalities.

Guide to Content Categories

Here is a guide on categorizing the content.

☐ 1 Performance outcomes, principles, key ideas ("application points")

☐ 2 Processes, tasks, steps, procedures

☐ 3 Tools, references, forms

☐ 4 People relationships and coordination

3-Minute e-Learning *Organic e-Learning Design*®

Appendix B

A   Structure of Content - Exercise # 1B
3-Minute e-Learning View

Presented below is an example of 3-Minute e-Learning content. (This is a fictitious table of contents for a program).

A program is needed to train bank tellers what to do in the event of a robbery.

10. **How to make sure everyone is safe, including you.** [1]

Answers below

People react to crisis in different ways. Some may panic at the sign of a threat, whereas others may stay calm and relaxed. In a hold-up situation, there are at least four groups of people: you, co-employees, the robber and your customers. Which person must you manage first? You! [4] [2]

Handling your own emotions is the starting point. How do you handle your emotions? Essentially, learning about your emotions ahead of time is the best way to learn to control them. Your emotions are heavily influenced by the amount of knowledge and information, and your attitudes in a crisis. If your instant reaction is to fight back, you could emotionally charge a crisis situation. You really cannot help others unless you are in control of yourself. [1] [1] [1] [1]

In the guide "How to handle stressful situations," you will find excellent tips on how to be in control. You may also visit the company counselor or view employee assistance programs if you wish to learn more about how you can master stressful situations. The FBI also issued an interesting article on studies of bank hold-ups. This study shows that most often, deaths or loss of life in hold-up situations are low, but there are practical steps to make sure that you avoid fatalities. [3] [4] [3]

Guide to Content Categories

Below is a guide on categorizing the content.

[1] Performance outcomes, principles, key ideas ("application points")

[2] Processes, tasks, steps, procedures

[3] Tools, references, forms

[4] People relationships and coordination

3-Minute e-Learning   *Organic e-Learning Design*®

A **Structure of Content - Exercise # 1C**

Application Exercise

This is a two-part exercise.

Part 1 - Macro View

Select and review the training outline of an existing training program from your organization. This is the program you may wish to convert into e-Learning.

From a macro view, identify the categories.

Part 2 - 3-Minute e-Learning View

Using the same content in Part 1 above, drill down to a granular content identified as a "performance outcomes" or application points category.

Review a few paragraphs and identify in the granular content the various categories.

Guide to Content Categories

Here is a guide on categorizing the content.

1 Performance outcomes, principles, key ideas ("application points")

2 Processes, tasks, steps, procedures

3 Tools, references, forms

4 People relationships and coordination

Step 1 - Analyzing and Categorizing Content

B **Analysis of Content - Identifying "MUST LEARNS"**

The next step after categorizing the content is to determine and isolate the "MUST LEARNS" content from secondary, reference or detailed knowledge. This is applying the 80/20 Rule: 20% produces 80% of the results.

After you have identified the performance outcomes, key principles and key ideas, test these content items to verify that they are "MUST LEARNS." "MUST LEARNS" are content that has very high impact on results, for which the learner needs the skills or "working proficiency" knowledge in order to successfully perform a task. Note that not all performance content are "MUST LEARNS."

Criteria for "MUST LEARNS"

Value - Do these topics impact sales, cash flow, cost cutting, customer service or quality? These are outcomes that could make a big difference.

Errors - Do these topics help learners avoid major errors, which if not corrected, could be damaging to the organization?

Difficulty - Do these topics cause so much frustration and inefficiencies because they are hard to learn or difficult to implement or use?

The benefits

Discovering the "MUST LEARNS":

1. Helps you further isolate those content items that impact completion of tasks and are significant contributions to results.

2. Allows you to focus on the 20% content that create 80% of the results.

Application Point or Performance Idea

10% of the 20% } **Must Learns**

20% {

80% {

Performance outcomes, application points principles, key ideas

Processes, tasks, steps, procedures

Tools, references, forms

People relationships and coordination

To fine tune further the usefulness of "application points," we need to identify the "Must Learns."

3-Minute e-Learning   *Organic e-Learning Design®*

Where to find application points in the content?

"Application points" may be found in each type of content. You may find "application points" in processes, tasks, forms and relationships.

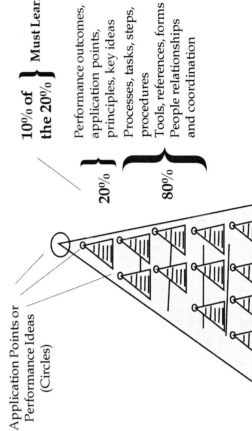

Application Points or Performance Ideas (Circles)

10% of the 20% } Must Learns

20%

80%

Performance outcomes, application points, principles, key ideas

Processes, tasks, steps, procedures

Tools, references, forms

People relationships and coordination

Application Points or Performance Ideas (Circles)

10% of the 20% } Must Learns

20%

80%

Performance outcomes, application points, principles, key ideas

Processes, tasks, steps, procedures

Tools, references, forms

People relationships and coordination

You may also find "application points" as performance ideas in groups of content. However, to get an aggregate number to estimate the content, it is likely that content has 20% as "Must Learn" and performance outcomes, while 80% is processes, steps, forms, etc.

3-Minute e-Learning   *Organic e-Learning Design*®

Step 1 - Analyzing and Categorizing Content

B

Analysis of Content - Exercise # 2A
The "MUST LEARNS" in 3-Minute e-Learning

Purpose: Using the bank teller training example, we developed, through exercises in the previous pages, understanding of the macro-view and 3-Minute e-Learning view of our learning content. We then learned how to isolate the "MUST LEARNS" from the body of content according to a 3-point criteria. The purpose of Exercise #2A is to learn to identify the "MUST LEARNS" from the content.

Activity: Study the granular content below and mark what ideas fall into "MUST LEARNS." Underline and put a corresponding number near the words or phrases in the content to correspond to the criteria.

Below is an example of a 3-Minute e-Learning.

A program is needed to train bank tellers what to do in the event of a robbery.

10. How to make sure everyone is safe, including you.

People react to crisis in different ways. Some will panic at the sign of a threat, whereas others may stay calm and relaxed. In a hold-up situation, there are at least four groups of people: you, co-employees, the robber and your customers. Which person must you manage first? You!

Handling your own emotions is the starting point. How do you handle your emotions? Essentially, learning about your emotions ahead of time is the best way to learn to control them. Your emotions are heavily influenced by the amount of knowledge and information, and your attitudes in a crisis.

If your instant reaction is to fight back others, you could emotionally charge a crisis situation. You really cannot help others unless you are in control of yourself.

In the guide "How to handle stressful situations," you will find excellent tips on how to be in control. You may also see the company counselor or view the employee assistance programs if you wish to learn more about how you can master stressful situations. The FBI also issued an interesting article on studies of bank hold-ups. This study shows that most often, deaths or loss of life in hold-up situations are low, but there are practical steps to make sure that you avoid fatalities.

Criteria for "Must Learns"

1 **Value** - Do these topics impact sales, cash flow, cost cutting, customer service or quality? These are outcomes that could make a big difference.

2 **Errors** - Do these topics help learners avoid major errors, and if not corrected could be damaging to the company?

3 **Difficulty** - Do these topics cause so much frustration and inefficiencies because they are hard to learn or difficult to implement or use?

3-Minute e-Learning   *Organic e-Learning Design*®

Step 1 - Analyzing and Categorizing Content

B Analysis of Content - Recap of Exercise # 2A
The "MUST LEARNS" in 3-Minute e-Learning

A program is needed to train bank tellers what to do in the event of a robbery.

10. How to make sure everyone is safe, including you.

People react to crisis in different ways. Some will panic at the sign of a threat, whereas others may stay calm and relaxed. In a hold-up situation, there are at least four groups of people: you, co-employees, the robber and your customers. Which person must you manage first?
You!

Answers below

Handling your own emotions is the starting point. How do you handle your emotions? Essentially, learning about your emotions ahead of time is the best way to learn to control them. [3]
Your emotions are heavily influenced by the amount of knowledge and information, and your attitudes in a crisis. If your instant reaction is to fight back others, you could emotion- [1] ally charge a crisis situation. You really cannot help others unless you are in control of yourself. [2]

In the guide "How to handle stressful situations," you will find excellent tips on how to be in control. You may also visit the company counselor or view employee assistance programs if you wish to learn more about how you can master stressful situations. The FBI also issued an interesting article on studies of bank hold-ups. This study shows that most often, deaths or loss of life in hold-up situations are low, but there are practical steps to make sure that you avoid fatalities.

Criteria for "Must Learns"

1 **Value** - Do these topics impact sales, cash flow, cost cutting, customer service or quality? These are outcomes that could make a big difference.

2 **Errors** - Do these topics help learners avoid major errors, and which if not corrected, could be damaging to the company?

3 **Difficulty** - Do these topics cause so much frustration and inefficiencies because they are hard to learn or difficult to implement or use?

3-Minute e-Learning   *Organic e-Learning Design*®

B Analysis of Content - Exercise # 2B

Application Exercise

Identifying "MUST LEARNS" in 3-Minute e-Learning

Purpose & Activity: Identify and use content from your organization or a content that you want to convert into e-Learning. You may use the same content from Exercise #1C. Drill down into the granular content which you identified to be in the "performance outcome" category. Review the paragraph(s) and identify the "MUST LEARNS."

Criteria for "MUST LEARNS"

1. **Value** - Do these topics impact sales, cash flow, cost cutting, customer service or quality? These are outcomes that could make a big difference.

2. **Errors** - Do these topics help learners avoid major errors, and if not corrected could be damaging to the company?

3. **Difficulty** - Do these topics cause so much frustration and inefficiencies because they are hard to learn or difficult to implement or use?

3-Minute e-Learning   *Organic e-Learning Design*®

Step 1 - Analyzing and Categorizing Content

C   Nature of Content - "Mechanics" and "Organics"

The nature of content consists of "Mechanics" and "Organics." Differentiate "MECHANICS" of the content, i.e. factual statement, description, functional, and structural from the "ORGANICS," i.e. stories, anecdotes, testimonials, examples, cases, and metaphors. Identify and discover the "Organics." You will need this differentiation to start improving the quality of your granular content.

Cause of boring and lifeless e-Learning programs

Often, the "Mechanics" are migrated into e-Learning, but the "Organics" are omitted. Consequently, many e-Learning programs, devoid of the human and emotional content, end up lifeless or boring. People learn best through "Organics" because, by nature, "Organics" add real-life context and meaning.

Criteria of good "Organics"

1. **Real-life** - is it based on experience?

2. **Emotional** - does it move people or touch people emotionally?

3. **Concrete** - is it observable and verifiable?

4. **Credible** - is it believable?

5. **Colorful, humorous** - does it inject the sense of the ridiculous and fun and entertainment when appropriate (but in good taste)?

6. **Meaningful** - does it allow people to relate to the content?

7. **Contextual** - does it help people to apply the mechanical information or perform a task?

The transformer of an idea into its application is the quality of the "Organics." Without "Organics," rapid application is hard to achieved.

The "Organics" transform or magnify the "application points" to real-life situations. They add context to the points.

Application Point or Performance Idea

10% of the 20% } Must Learns

20%

Performance outcomes, principles, key ideas

"Organics"

3-Minute e-Learning   Organic e-Learning Design®

Methods for "Organics"

Essentially, at the heart of "Organics" is a story. A story, in its variety of forms and its related methods, transforms or accompanies the "Mechanics" content, thereby making it accessible for people to experience.

Following are methods of the "Organics":

1. **Stories** - relating of incidents or events; a statement regarding the facts pertinent to a situation in question.

2. **Anecdotes** - usually short narratives of interesting, amusing or biographical incidents.

3. **Case studies** - recording of history, environment and relevant details of a case especially for use in analysis or illustration.

4. **Examples** - parallel or closely similar cases especially when serving as precedents or models.

5. **Illustrations/demonstrations** - to provide with visual features intended to explain; to make clear.

6. **Metaphors** - figures of speech in which a word or phrase literally denoting one kind of object or idea is used in place of another to suggest a likeness or analogy between them.

The function of "Organics" in 3-Minute e-Learning and rapid application of application points

Good "Organics" and the appropriate methods can help learners immediately apply knowledge, ideas and principles. "Organics" elevate the "Mechanics" into meaningful and easily applicable knowledge, ideas or skills. The transformer of an idea into its application is the quality of the "Organics." Without "Organics," rapid application is hard to achieve. "Organics" work like step-up electrical transformers. They raise the power of the mechanical or factual information or increase its usefulness and learning value.

3-Minute e-Learning   *Organic e-Learning Design*®

Methods of "Organics" match type of learning required

The chart below illustrates the possible relationships that exist between the type of learning required and the methods of "Organics." **Note:** In each type of learning required, one dominant method may work best. However, a combination of methods may overlap to create good "Organics."

Types of learning required	a. Stories	b. Anecdotes	c. Case studies	d. Examples	e. Illustrations/ demonstrations	f. Metaphors
1. Emotional, decision-making, calling judgement, e.g. leadership training	✓					
2. Technical, manual-handling, e.g. equipment handling					✓	
3. Relationship, requires person-to-person interaction, e.g. sales and customer service, coaching	✓					
4. Software, e.g. Oracle software				✓		
5. Conceptual, theoretical, e.g. equations, formulas			✓			
6. Action-oriented, tasks and goals outcome, e.g. knowledge for quick reference		✓				
7. Compliance, background, historical, e.g. HIPAA, OSHA, Wage and Hour		✓				

Methods →

3-Minute e-Learning   *Organic e-Learning Design*®

How and where to collect good "Organics"?

1. Participants or workers - they are rich with experiences on the uses or applications of ideas.

2. Case histories - records of past problems, e.g. phone logs, service call records, investigations, etc.

3. Successes or failures/best practices - documented practices

4. Subject Matter Experts (SMEs) - they can assist in the development of "Organics" for e-Learning programs within their expertise.

Simple ways to find a good story

A simple way to find a story is to ask the following questions. The answers are usually already good "Organics."

1. What can really go wrong or what can really go right or successfully if the idea is applied or not applied?

2. What are the benefits or the risks?

3. What is the upside or downside or the advantages and disadvantages?

4. What are the consequences, bad or good?

5. What are the impacts to your work?

6. How would you use this in a real-life situation?

7. How would you use this idea to solve problems or make things better?

Please see Appendix C for the SME Interview Guide.

3-Minute e-Learning *Organic e-Learning Design*®

Steps in creating the "Organics"

The following steps help you create the appropriate "Organics" for a 3-Minute e-Learning:

1. Identify the "Mechanics" and "Organics" of the 3-Minute e-Learning.

2. Match the content with the right "Organics" method.

3. Ask the questions to obtain stories or details to strengthen the "Organics."

4. Select and write the "Organics."

5. Test the selected "Organics" according to the criteria of good "Organics."

3-Minute e-Learning   *Organic e-Learning Design*®

Step 1 - Analyzing and Categorizing Content

C Nature of Content - "Mechanics" and "Organics" - Exercise #3A

Differentiating the "Organics" from the "Mechanics" in 3-Minute e-Learning

Purpose: The content below is the same bank teller training situation which we studied in Exercises #1 and #2. The purpose of this exercise is to identify the "Organics" or detect their absence and differentiate them from the "Mechanics."

Activity: You may wish to underline and put a corresponding number near the words or phrases in the content to correspond to the "Organics" or "Mechanics."

A program is needed to train bank tellers what to do in the event of a robbery.

10. How to make sure everyone is safe, including you. (Granular content below).

People react to crisis in different ways. Some may panic at the sign of a threat, whereas others may stay calm and relaxed. In a hold-up situation, there are at least four groups of people: you, co-employees, the robber and your customers. Which person must you manage first? You!

Jane, a branch teller, shares her experience. "I have always been a very in-control type of person. My confidence is high, and I never lost my cool until the terrible day of the hold-up." She continues, "I thought I could withstand the tension. I caved in and panicked. I cried like a little baby! It only shows that I really didn't know that part of me, until I was in the situation."

Handling your own emotions is a challenge, but this is the starting point. How do you handle your emotions? Essentially, learning about your emotions ahead of time is the best way to learn to control them. Your emotions are heavily influenced by the amount of knowledge and information, and your attitudes in a crisis. If your instant reaction is to fight back, you could emotionally charge a crisis situation. You really cannot help others unless you are in control of yourself.

In the guide "How to handle stressful situations," you will find excellent tips on how to be in control. You may also visit and see the company counselor or view employee assistance programs if you wish to learn more about how you can master stressful situations. The FBI also issued an interesting article on studies of bank hold-ups. The article states that most often deaths or loss of life in hold-up situations are low, but there are practical steps to make sure that you avoid fatalities.

1 "MECHANICS" - factual statement, description, functional, and structural. Identify and discover the "Mechanics."

2 "ORGANICS" - stories, anecdotes, testimonials, examples, cases, metaphors. Identify and discover the "Organics."

 Appendix **B**

3-Minute e-Learning   *Organic e-Learning Design*®

Match the content with the right "Organics" method – Exercise #3B

Purpose: The content below is the same bank teller training situation which we studied in Exercises #1 and #2. Identify the "Organics" or detect their absence and differentiate them from the "Mechanics."

Activity: Using the granular content from the Exercise #3A, do the following: (1) encircle below the type of learning required of the bank teller training granular content; (2) put a check mark under the appropriate method you have selected.

Methods	a. Stories	b. Anecdotes	c. Case studies	d. Examples	e. Illustrations/ demonstrations	f. Metaphors
Types of learning required						
1. Emotional, decision-making, calling judgement, e.g. leadership training						
2. Technical, manual-handling, e.g. equipment handling						
3. Relationship, requires person-to-person interaction, e.g. sales and customer service, coaching						
4. Software, e.g. Oracle software						
5. Conceptual, theoretical, e.g. equations, formulas						
6. Action-oriented, tasks and goals outcome, e.g. knowledge for quick reference						
7. Compliance, background, historical, e.g. HIPAA, OSHA, Wage and Hour						

3-Minute e-Learning   *Organic e-Learning Design* ®

Create, build, and test the "Organics" – Exercise #3C

Purpose: In this exercise your task is to complete an example of "Organics" for the bank teller training program granular content.

Activity: Using the granular content from the Exercise #3A, do the following:

1. Ask the questions to obtain stories or details to strengthen the "Organics."

2. Select and write the "Organics."

3. Test the selected "Organics" according to the criteria for good "Organics."

Refer to the previous pages for the detailed guides.

At the end of the exercise you will present the "Organics" you created.

3-Minute e-Learning   *Organic e-Learning Design*®

Develop the "Organics" for your own 3-Minute e-Learning - Exercise #3D

Application Exercise

Purpose & Activity: Identify and use content from your organization or content that you want to convert into e-Learning. You may use the same content in Exercise #2B. Apply the steps in creating the "Organics."

Steps in creating the "Organics"

The following steps help you create the appropriate "Organics" for a granular content.

1. Identify the "Mechanics" and "Organics" of the granular content.

2. Match the content with the right "Organics" method.

3. Ask the questions to obtain stories or details to strengthen the "Organics."

4. Select and write the "Organics."

5. Test the selected "Organics" according to the criteria of good "Organics."

5-Step Development Process - Review Page

These are the details of each step.

Steps 1 and 2 fall under **Organic Design Decisions**

Steps 3, 4, and 5 fall under **Organic Production Process**

1 Analyzing and Categorizing Content

Breaking down content into organized and relevant parts and pieces. This categorization helps trainers lay out content on lesson pages to enable learners to have better control of the learning process.

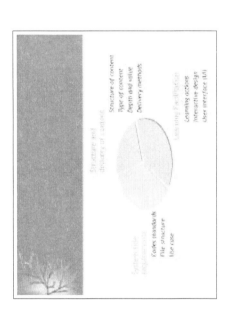

2 Developing Lesson Pages

The content is laid out on the appropriate type of pages with relationship of thought and content carefully considered to ensure that learning starts with "must learn" topics and then moves to "in-depth and detailed" content. Covered here are: **Laying out pages, and writing and designing e-Learning programs.**

3 Developing Interface and Interactive Design

The content and the pages are tested and converted into a schematic that guides in the development of navigation, flow and relationships of the different elements.

4 Selecting The Methods and Tools

This process allows trainers to evaluate and assess the types of tools and methods they wish to employ to achieve the program goals.

5 Preparing Budgets and Documentation for Lesson Pages

This final step helps trainers and developers convey their design into documentation that contains the features, functions and systems requirements as well as the costing and timing. This step bridges the e-Learning process to software selection and development process.

3-Minute e-Learning   *Organic e-Learning Design* ®

5-Step Development Process

2 ## Developing Lesson Pages in 3-Minute e-Learning

After categorizing the content, we now move into laying out the basic design of a simple "3-Minute e-Learning" lesson, snippet, nugget or vignette.

The content is laid out on the appropriate type of pages with relationship of thought and content carefully considered to ensure that learning starts with "must learn" topics, then moves to "in-depth and detailed" content.

Supporting 3-Minute e-Learning and e-Learning Behaviors

The approach in page layout encourages or supports e-Learning Behaviors. The layout supports:

1. Focus on quick access to performance content ("application points")
2. Easy entries and exits
3. Random usage of the content
4. Quick problem-solving
5. Easy access to content that meets learner needs

Covered in these sections are the following topics:
Page layouts, writing and assembling 3-Minute e-Learning granular content, a small lesson, snippet, nugget or vignette

As a review, Step 2 falls under Organic Design Decisions in the Organic e-Learning Design Process

Steps 1 and 2 fall under
Organic Design Decisions

Steps 3, 4 and 5 fall under
Organic Production Process

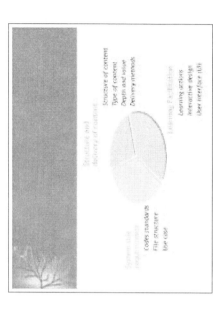

3-Minute e-Learning   *Organic e-Learning Design*®

Step 2 - Developing Lesson Pages - Content Hierarchy

Understanding Content Hierarchy in 3-Minute e-Learning

Developing lesson pages starts with the content hierarchy of your program, i.e. module and lesson topics, chapters or sections or a table of contents. A lesson is the smallest element, a granule or a 3-Minute e-Learning.

For example, one way to organize the sequence of content is using the Module-Lesson-Review Flow.

Modules *(m1)*
(There may be several modules or chapters)

Lessons (There may be several lessons in a module)
(The opposite image is a lesson structure)
(l1)

Main Pages *(p1 - 14)*
Jump Pages   *(j1)* - **Link Pages** *(lp1)*

Lesson Review Pages

Module Review Pages

The items: *(m1)* signifies module number, *(l1 - l4)* signifies the lesson number *(p1)* signifies the page number, *(j1)* signifies the jump page number and *(lp1)* signifies the link page number.

Important: Although we speak of program, modules, lessons, and pages, ideally the 3-Minute e-Learning lesson, snippet, nugget, or vignette should be stand-alone content. So they can stand alone when not presented with the whole program, module and lesson structure.

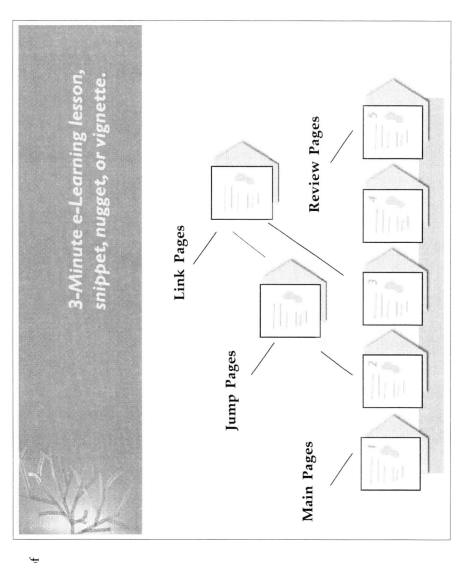

3-Minute e-Learning lesson, snippet, nugget, or vignette.

Link Pages

Jump Pages

Review Pages

Main Pages

Ideally, a 3-Minute e-Learning is a stand alone, independent, flexible, movable, and transferable learning object.

Step 2 - Developing Lesson Pages - Laying Out Content On 3-Minute e-Learning

Laying out pages involves making decisions on why, where and how particular content and activities should go to specific pages.

1

Main pages and basic structure

A 3-Minute e-Learning lesson is a small set of content that participants can learn in a few minutes - **3 minutes more or less**, or longer, depending on the participants' specific and current learning need and interests. Lessons allow quick entry and exit or quick access to details provided in links.

For example, found in main pages are 30-50 words of performance goals, application points, key ideas, principles, "Must Learn" ideas, (80/20), that is.

Page 1 - Introduction, gaining attention, "Organics"
Page 2 - Application points, goals, key ideas
Page 3 - Key principles
Page 4 - Introducing a detailed idea
Page 5 - Review page

The lesson pages may also display interactivity, i.e. simulation or an exercise.

Page 1 - Login screen presented (learner has to login)
Page 2 - Create accounts (learner action)
Page 3 - Enter names of prospects (learner action)
Page 4 - Enter company profile; save (learner action)
Page 5 - Preview to check accuracy (learner gets feedback)

Lessons may cover learning ideas (content), exercises (interactivity) or assignments and OJT (applications), and module reviews (learning reflections).

Definition of a page

A page consists of the total view presented in a screen. It may be a web page or a page in an interactive simulation, slideshow, PowerPoint or video.

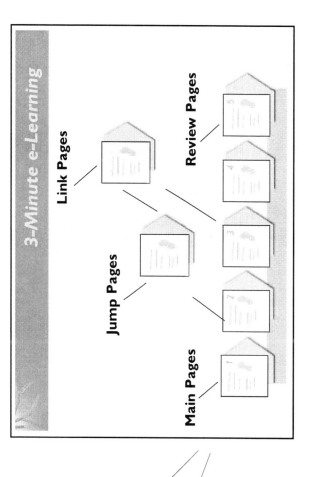

3-Minute e-Learning

Main Pages   Jump Pages   Link Pages   Review Pages

3-Minute e-Learning   Organic e-Learning Design®

Below is an illustration of how the "application point" pyramid relates to layout of pages. The "application points" are positioned in main pages, while secondary content is placed as links.

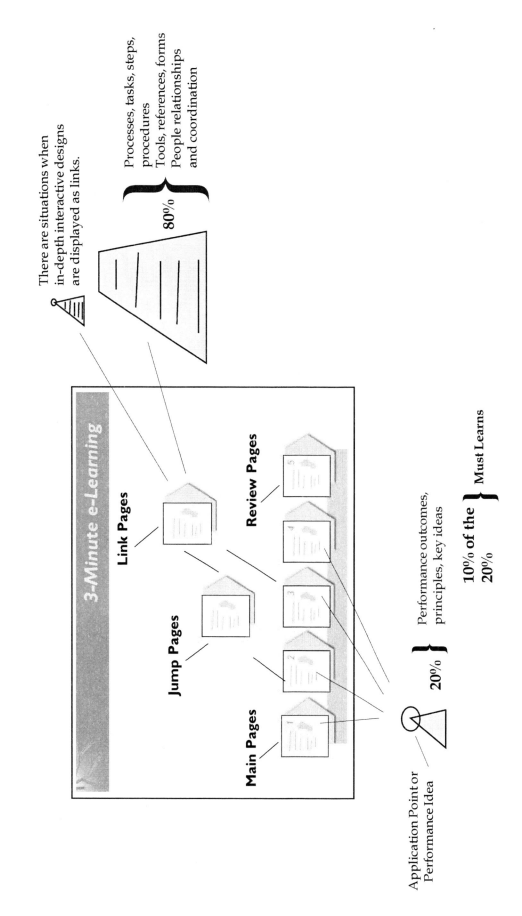

There are situations when in-depth interactive designs are displayed as links.

Processes, tasks, steps, procedures
Tools, references, forms
People relationships and coordination

80%

3-Minute e-Learning

Link Pages

Jump Pages

Main Pages

Review Pages

Application Point or Performance Idea

20%

Performance outcomes, principles, key ideas

10% of the 20% } Must Learns

3-Minute e-Learning   *Organic e-Learning Design*®

2 **Jump Pages**

Jump pages are pages that summarize or introduce links that contain references. For example, before you present an HTML page or a PDF page with over 2,000 words on a company policy, you may need to show first a page that tells the learner what to look for in the HTML or PDF page. So, instead of being lost in the 2,000 words of the PDF, the learners are logically guided.

Jump pages help learners get an overview of instruction on how to review or what to focus on in the link pages, especially when the link pages contain a great amount of text or references.

With the use of jump pages learners save time, accelerate their study, and reduce the frustration that often arises when navigating the volumes of pages or content.

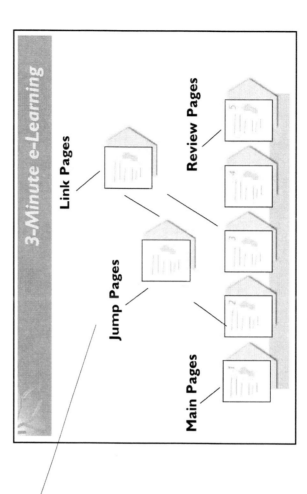

3-Minute e-Learning

Jump Pages

Link Pages

Main Pages

Review Pages

Step 2 - Developing Lesson Pages - Laying Out Content On 3-Minute e-Learning

3 **Link Pages**

Link Pages contain detailed information on processes, tasks, steps, procedures, tools, references, forms, people and relationships. Several methods are used, e.g. download, PowerPoint, Word Document, Excel, PDF manual, assignments, OJT and others.

Links to interactivity, media, discussions, WIKIs, collaboration tools, etc.
Link pages are also links to in-depth content. These types of links allow learners to drill down to more content to support learning or find more answers and solutions. Several methods are used such as download, HTML, XML, PowerPoint, Word Document, Excel, PDF Manual, assignments, OJT and others. Usually content that are intended for "**full proficiencies**" are delivered in links.

3-Minute e-Learning

Link Pages

Jump Pages

Main Pages

Review Pages

Step 2 - Developing Lesson Pages - Laying Out Content On 3-Minute e-Learning

4 **Review Page(s)**

Each lesson ends with a review page. A review page is for learning reflection or application. It is different from an assessment or certification test, which measures retention or understanding. This can also be placed in the middle of a lesson to help participants reflect or interact with the content, coach or peers.

Review pages contain the programming codes to capture some form of tracking.

Review pages should not be confused with assessment tests. If we put assessment tests in a lesson, they distract the learner. They are best presented at the end of the program or a series of modules. Assessment tests meet the needs of trainers and administrators, but do not support learner needs.

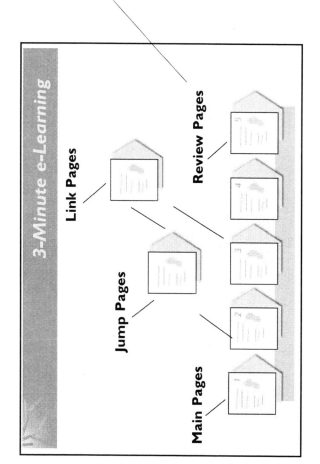

Step 2 - Developing Lesson Pages - Writing and Designing for 3-Minute e-Learning

In writing and designing content include the following styles, tools, and techniques.

5 **From the very start, write in the "Organics" tone.**

In e-Learning, one of the basic challenges is to design programs for learners with short attention spans or who multi-task. Unless the lesson pages grab the attention of learners in the first few seconds, we lose the opportunity to keep the learners' interest.

To solve this problem, write the lesson pages with "Organics" in mind.

Weave the content into a story, anecdote, case study or other forms of "Organics."

Write in an informal tone. State the benefits for participants. Use "Organics" to intro-duce the content. Write the text, prepare the graphics and include other elements to heighten the "Organics."

Link Pages

Jump Pages

Review Pages

Main Pages

Module   Links

Lesson

Title

text text text   graphics

text text text

text text text

text text text

Directions   Links

6 **Basic structure of a page**

Each page has about fifty words and is accompanied by an image. The image (graphics) should reflect the ideas in the text. Directions are provided and links are apparent.

3-Minute e-Learning *Organic e-Learning Design*®

Step 2 - Developing Lesson Pages - Writing and Designing Content

7 **Facilitate Learning - Use directions smartly and maintain a "conversation" with your learners.**

Use directions and user interface (UI) design to facilitate, guide, coach and prod participants to study the content. Examples of maintaining a conversation are: "Click to see the benefits," "Study the example," "Reflect on this for a moment," "What would you do?," "Click to discover," "Click to learn more," etc.

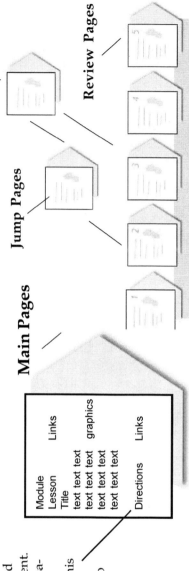

Link Pages

Jump Pages

Review Pages

Main Pages

Module		Links
Lesson		
Title		
text text text		graphics
text text text		
text text text		
text text text		
Directions		Links

Step 2 - Developing Lesson Pages - Writing and Designing for 3-Minute e-Learning

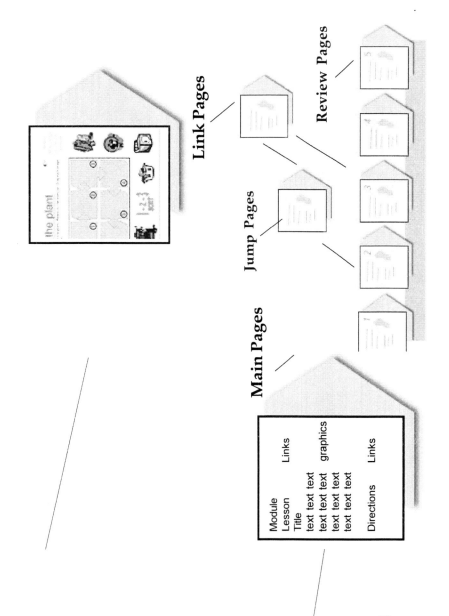

Link Pages

Jump Pages

Review Pages

Main Pages

Module		Links
Lesson		
Title		
text text text		graphics
text text text		
text text text		
text text text		
Directions		Links

8

In-depth interactivity

Links within lessons may consist of in-depth interactivity, i.e. games, simulation, role-playing, assessments, etc.

Interactivity may also cover links to a virtual classroom, discussion room, chat room, Instant Messaging, WIKI, blog, and others.

Five types of interactive design
1. Knowledge Mapping
2. Rote Learning
3. Technical Training
4. Judgment and Decision-Making Learning
5. Emotional and Behavioral Learning

9

Basic and advanced interactive design

The basic lesson design and layout is the most basic interactive format, while in-depth interactivity consists of advanced interactive designs.

3-Minute e-Learning   *Organic e-Learning Design*®

Step 2 - Developing Lesson Pages - Writing and Designing for 3-Minute e-Learning

When is in-depth interactivity employed?

In situations where in-depth interactivity is required, the interactivity is focused on the "MUST LEARNS." The interactivity, therefore, may represent only the 10% of the 20% "application points" where value is required, errors often occur, and the content is difficult to learn or apply.

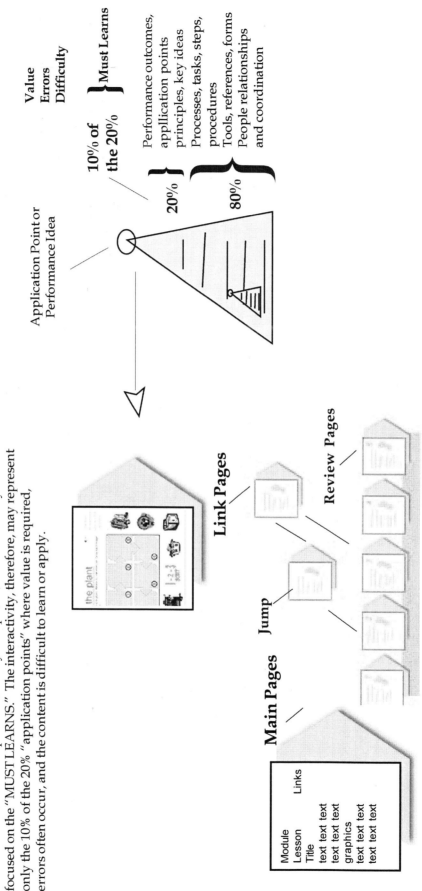

Application Point or Performance Idea

10% of the 20% } Must Learns

Value
Errors
Difficulty

20% }

80% } Performance outcomes, appllication points principles, key ideas
Processes, tasks, steps, procedures
Tools, references, forms
People relationships and coordination

Main Pages   Jump

Link Pages

Review Pages

Module   Links
Lesson
Title
text text text
text text text
graphics
text text text
text text text

Appendix B

Step 2 - Developing Lesson Pages - Writing and Designing for 3-Minute e-Learning

C Applying Basic Layout - Exercise #4A

Purpose: The content below is the same bank teller training example we studied in Exercises #1 and #2. Use this content and apply the basic lesson design process. Apply ideas from numbers (1) to (7), Step 2 - Developing Lesson Pages.

Activity: Study the content below and lay out a lesson. Use the form in the next page.

A program is needed to train bank tellers what to do in the event of a robbery.

10. How to make sure everyone is safe, including you? (Granular content below).

People react to crisis in different ways. Some may panic at the sign of a threat, whereas others may stay calm and relaxed. In a hold-up situation, there are at least four groups of people: you, co-employees, the robber and your customers. Which person must you manage first? You!

Jane, a branch teller, shares her experience. "I have always been a very in-control type of person. My confidence is high, and I never lost my cool until the terrible day of the hold-up." She continues, "I thought I could withstand the tension. I caved in and panicked. I cried like a little baby! It only shows that I really didn't know that part of me, until I was in the situation."

Handling your own emotions is a challenge, but this is the starting point. How do you handle your emotions?

Essentially, learning about your emotions ahead of time is the best way to learn to control them. Your emotions are heavily influenced by the amount of knowledge and information, and your attitudes in a crisis. If your instant reaction is to fight back others, you could emotionally charge a crisis situation. You really cannot help unless you are in control of yourself.

In the guide "How to handle stressful situations," you will find excellent tips on how to be in control. You may also visit the company counselor or view employee assistance programs if you wish to learn more about how you can master stressful situations. The FBI also issued an interesting article on studies of bank hold-ups. This study shows that most often deaths or loss of life in hold-up situations are low, but there are practical steps to make sure that you avoid fatalities.

_____
_____
_____
_____
_____
_____
_____
_____

3-Minute e-Learning   *Organic e-Learning Design*®

Exercise #4A: Step 2 - Developing Lesson Pages (Exercise Page)

Using the form below, apply ideas from numbers (1) to (7), Step 2 - Developing Lesson Pages.

1 Main Pages

_____

_____

_____

_____

_____

_____

2 Jump Pages

_____

_____

_____

3 Link Pages

_____

_____

_____

4 Review Page(s)

_____

_____

_____

3-Minute e-Learning

Link Pages

Jump Pages

Main Pages

Review Pages

3-Minute e-Learning   *Organic e-Learning Design*®

Exercise #4A: Step 2 - Developing Lesson Pages (Exercise Page)

Using the form below, apply ideas from numbers (1) to (7), Step 2 - Developing Lesson Pages.

1 Main Pages

_____

_____

_____

_____

_____

2 Jump Pages

_____

_____

3 Link Pages

_____

_____

4 Review Page(s)

_____

_____

_____

3-Minute e-Learning

Link Pages

Jump Pages

Main Pages

Review Pages

Appendix B

Exercise #4B: Step 2 - Developing Lesson Pages - Using Your Own Granular Content

Use your own example of granular content. Lay out your content into a lesson design. Apply ideas from numbers (1) to (7), Step 2 - Developing Lesson Pages.

1 Main Pages

_____

_____

_____

_____

_____

2 Jump Pages

_____

_____

_____

_____

_____

3 Link Pages

_____

_____

_____

_____

_____

4 Review Page(s)

_____

_____

_____

_____

_____

3-Minute e-Learning

Link Pages

Jump Pages

Main Pages

Review Pages

Exercise #4B: Step 2 - Developing Lesson Pages - Using Your Own Granular Content

Use your own example of granular content. Lay out your content into a lesson design. Apply ideas from numbers (1) to (7), Step 2 - Developing Lesson Pages.

1 Main Pages

_____

_____

_____

_____

_____

2 Jump Pages

_____

_____

_____

3 Link Pages

_____

_____

_____

_____

4 Review Page(s)

_____

_____

_____

3-Minute e-Learning

Link Pages

Jump Pages

Main Pages

Review Pages

3-Minute e-Learning   *Organic e-Learning Design*®

Exercise #4C: Step 2 - Developing Lesson Pages - Using Lesson Worksheets

Purpose: Use your own content. Identify a very small lesson (one key idea or a subset of an idea). Analyze and categorize the content using the learning points on the previous pages. Use the worksheets provided in this exercise. You may need several worksheets to complete several pages for a small lesson.

Follow the form in the worksheet_example.doc provided in the link below. Download the form worksheet_example.doc from the reference web site.

Benefit of the exercise: The exercise helps you learn how to convert your content into a document or worksheet. This document will contain all the details you want to see in your modules, lessons and pages. By doing this exercise, you are preparing a document (others call this storyboarding) which you will provide to your developers. This helps developers execute your instructional design.

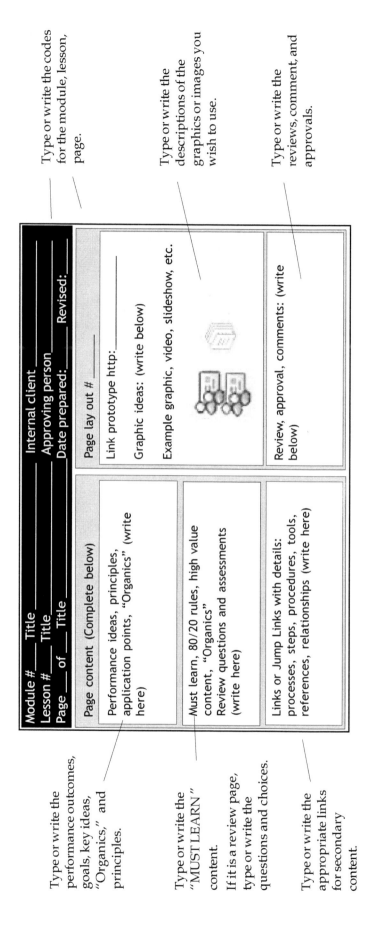

Type or write the codes for the module, lesson, page.

Type or write the descriptions of the graphics or images you wish to use.

Type or write the reviews, comment, and approvals.

Type or write the performance outcomes, goals, key ideas, "Organics," and principles.

Type or write the "MUST LEARN" content.
If it is a review page, type or write the questions and choices.

Type or write the appropriate links for secondary content.

Form content:

Module # _____ Title _____
Lesson # _____ Title _____
Page _____ of _____ Title _____

Page content (Complete below)

Performance ideas, principles, application points, "Organics" (write here)

Must learn, 80/20 rules, high value content, "Organics"
Review questions and assessments (write here)

Links or Jump Links with details: processes, steps, procedures, tools, references, relationships (write here)

Internal client _____
Approving person _____
Date prepared: _____   Revised: _____

Page lay out # _____

Link prototype http: _____

Graphic ideas: (write below)

Example graphic, video, slideshow, etc.

Review, approval, comments: (write below)

3-Minute e-Learning
Organic e-Learning Design Process

Review of the major components

Steps 1 and 2 fall under Organic Content Development Process

Steps 3, 4 and 5 fall under Organic Production Process
Presented in the next section

Step 3 - Developing Interface & Interactive Design

The next step in the process is the development of an interactive flow or model of your lesson design.

Interactive flow - testing the learning experience

You now make a drawing of your content pages with special attention to testing the learning flow, logic, relationships of elements, interactivity, learning time, difficulty, ease and convenience, and language of navigation. Interface design focuses on "how well the elements perform to achieve the intended outcome."

Systems, functions, structure and file conventions

Simultaneously, you capture the systems and functions definitions of your design, i.e. navigation, file conventions, graphical elements and data tracking.

Developing templates or models for interactive flow

In this step you are designing the interactive flow of a lesson. You may eventually develop several models and templates. Each model or template will be a pattern for designing lessons with interactive links, reviews and tests, self-assessments, homework or assignments, on-the-job follow-up, video and virtual classroom links, help and reference links, and others. The objective is to create models that you can use as patterns for all other designs.

For example, you may have a model for lessons that is highly interactive using Captivate or SimWriter, a simple and basic reference lesson, a lesson with blended interaction with off-line activity and assessments, and many other models.

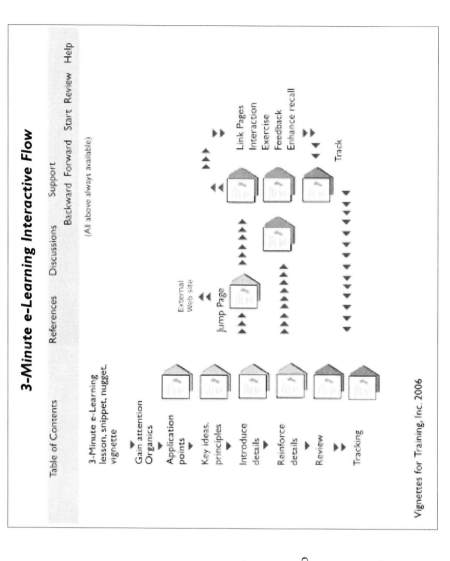

3-Minute e-Learning *Interactive Flow*

Vignettes for Training, Inc. 2006

3-Minute e-Learning   *Organic e-Learning Design*®

Step 3 - Developing Interface & Interactive Design

Part of developing an interactive flow of your content pages is creating a diagram flow of the "software behavior."

Interactive flow - navigation flow

Another way of explaining the interactive model or flow is by developing a diagram of the navigation flow or the behavior of the software. The diagram helps you explain to your programmers or developers the flow or navigation of your lesson.

NOTE: The illustration in this page is not related or similar to the one on any previous pages.

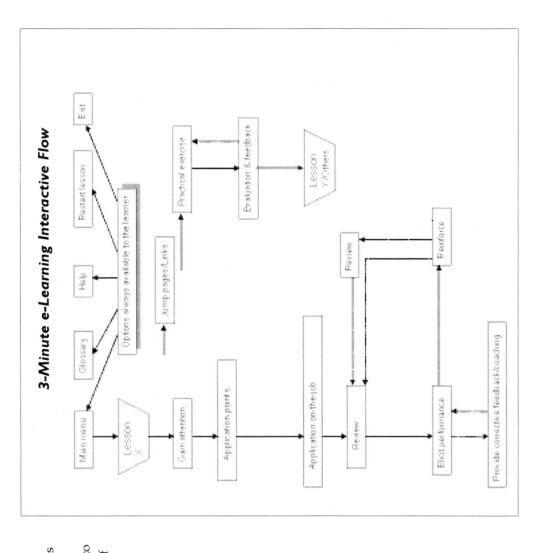

3-Minute e-Learning Interactive Flow

Step 4 - Selecting Delivery Methods for 3-Minute e-Learning

In this process you select the right methods and tools to deliver your lessons.

The various e-Learning methods, tools and resources

While you are developing your lesson pages and interactive flow, you should also be selecting what e-Learning methods support your delivery.

The following are considerations in selecting which method works for you based on your performance objectives, timelines, budgets, skills and talent at your disposal.

For rapid development, it is important that as you gain more experience, you collect data on each method:

1. The contribution of the tool
2. How it works
3. The cost of acquiring the tool
4. Time to develop
5. Type of skills needed
6. The software required and its costs
7. How to produce or use them rapidly
8. Technologies that require external support
9. Cost of maintenance

Overall, you need to be able to sum up the cost and time impact of each tool.

e-Learning Methods, Tools, and Resources

Presenting Content	Retaining Knowledge	Developing Skills	Enabling Competency
Multimedia	**Rote Interaction**	**On-the-job Training**	**Just-in-time Performance Support**
text	tests	assignments	search
graphic	exercises	job practice	bookmark
audio	feedback	apprenticeship	email URL
video	profiles	internship	journal/note taking
slideshow	assessments	mentoring	personalization
help / references	certifications	coaching	skills inventory
PDFs		projects	email alerts
HMTL	**Self-discovery Interaction**	informal learning	collaboration
XML	simulation		learning communities
	storytelling		WIKIs
	case studies		blogs
	scenario-based		social networking
			mobile
	People Interaction		performance metrics
	chat rooms		Dynanic ADDIE
	discussion rooms		
	listservs		
	email		
	instant messaging		
	texting		
	virtual classroom		

3-Minute e-Learning   *Organic e-Learning Design*®

Step 4 - Selecting Delivery Methods for 3-Minute e-Learning

Matching the type of content with the appropriate e-Learning tools

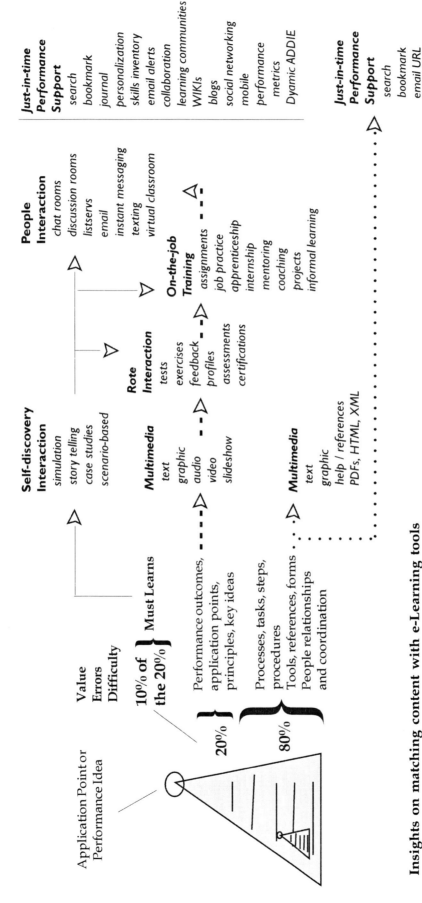

Application Point or Performance Idea

Value
Errors
Difficulty

10% of the 20%   } Must Learns

20%

Performance outcomes, application points, principles, key ideas

80%

Processes, tasks, steps, procedures
Tools, references, forms
People relationships and coordination

Self-discovery Interaction
simulation
story telling
case studies
scenario-based

Multimedia
text
graphic
audio
video
slideshow

Rote Interaction
tests
exercises
feedback
profiles
assessments
certifications

People Interaction
chat rooms
discussion rooms
listservs
email
instant messaging
texting
virtual classroom

On-the-job Training
assignments
job practice
apprenticeship
internship
mentoring
coaching
projects
informal learning

Just-in-time Performance Support
search
bookmark
journal
personalization
skills inventory
email alerts
collaboration
learning communities
WIKIs
blogs
social networking
mobile
performance
metrics
Dyamic ADDIE

Multimedia
text
graphic
help / references
PDFs, HTML, XML

Just-in-time Performance Support
search
bookmark
email URL
journal/note taking
email alerts

Insights on matching content with e-Learning tools

1. The top 10% of 20%, the MUST LEARNs, and the 20% performance outcomes content require high-end interactivity including self-discovery, people interaction, and on-the-job training. These tools are usually costly and takes time to develop.

2. The bulk of the content, which is (80%), is usually presented in text, graphics, help and reference guides, HTML, XML, PDFS, Word, and Excel documents. These tools are usually inexpensive. To help learners quickly access content in this area, the following tools may be added: search engines, bookmarks, journals, email reminders, and others.

3-Minute e-Learning   Organic e-Learning Design®

Step 5 - Preparing Budgets and Documentation for 3-Minute e-Learning

Preparing Budgets and Documentation for 3-Minute e-Learning

This final step helps trainers and developers convey their design into documentation that embodies the initial list of features, functions, systems requirements and the costing and timing. This step bridges the e-Learning process to software selection and development process.

1. Under methods, select the types of methods you plan to use for each lesson page.

2. Total the number of units of each method for each lesson.

3. Estimate the cost and time needed. Repeat the process for all the lessons, snippets, nuggets, or vignette you plan to produce and sum up the total program costs and timelines.

4. Make a decision as to whether the cost and timelines are acceptable or not. You can repeat the process in order to fine tune the design (deleting parts, using another method, using another producer or vendor or improving a process of production), the budget and timelines.

5. The estimates and specifics for each module and lesson become part of your RFI/P (Request for Information or Proposal).

Estimated costs and timing

Title: _____

Lesson: _____

Lesson Pages	Page 1	Page 2	Page 3	Page 4	Page 5	Review Page	Total
Methods (below are examples)							
Text/HTML	1	1	1	1	1	1	6
Images	1	1	1	1			4
Link PDF				1			1
Video link (1 min)					1		1
Simulation link			1				1
(add more items if needed)							

Illustration:

1. Text/HTML	6 (75 words)	x $5 total of	$ 30.00	1 hour
2. Images	4 (photos)	x $45 total of	$ 180.00	4 hours
3. Link PDF	1 (text)	x 10 total of	$ 10.00	1 hour
4. Video (1 min)	1 (high quality)	x $500 total of	$ 500.00	5 days
5. Simulation	1 (5 min)	x $2,000 total of	$2,000.00	2 weeks

Grand total $2,720.00   2 weeks (time span)

Time span of time is dependent on how many people are involved in the project and the complexity of the design.

Appendix B

Step 5 - Preparing Budgets and Documentation for 3-Minute e-Learning

Purpose of the final documentation

The documentation helps you communicate with developers or vendors about your e-Learning content design, the methods and tools, and the budget and timelines for your project.

The process of Organic e-Learning Design ensures that your developers and vendors have a clear guide and specifics to follow. This helps in making sure your programs meet the quality, cost and timeline objectives.

Checklist of Documentation

1. Design layout for all modules, lessons and pages using the *worksheets*.
   This encompasses all the elements in a lesson including the **methods, tools and resources.**

2. **Interactive flow** template for each lesson including the diagram of software behavior.

3. **Budgeting and timeline** document showing budgets for each module and lesson and the time allotted for each lesson.

3-Minute e-Learning   *Organic e-Learning Design*®

5-Step Development Process - Review and Concluding Page

These are the details of each step.

Steps 1 and 2 fall under
Organic Design Decisions

Steps 3, 4 and 5 fall under
Organic Production Process

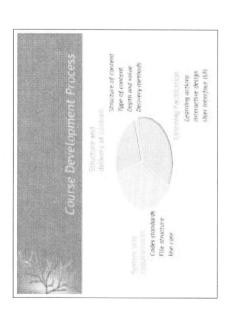

1 **Analyzing and Categorizing Content**

Breaking down content into organized and relevant parts and pieces. This categorization helps trainers lay out content on lesson pages to enable learners to have better control of the learning process.

2 **Developing Lesson Pages**

The content is laid out on the appropriate type of pages with relationship of thought and content carefully considered to ensure that learning starts with "must learn" topics and then moves to "in-depth and detailed" content. Covered here are: **Laying out pages, and writing and designing e-learning programs.**

3 **Developing Interface and Interactive Design**

The content and the pages are tested and converted into a schematic that guides in the development of navigation, flow and relationships of the different elements.

4 **Selecting The Methods and Tools**

This process allows trainers to evaluate and assess the types of tools and methods they wish to employ to achieve the program goals.

5 **Preparing Budgets and Documentation for Lesson Pages**

This final step helps trainers and developers convey their design into documentation that contains the features, functions and systems requirements, as well as the costing and timing. This step bridges the e-Learning process to software selection and development process.

Copyright 2006   www.vignettestraining.com   *Organic e-Learning Design Process* ®   Apendix B-57

3-Minute e-Learning   *Organic e-Learning Design* ®

End. Nothing follows.

3-Minute e-Learning
Subject Matter Expert (SME) Interview Guide
Ray E. Jimenez, Ph.D.

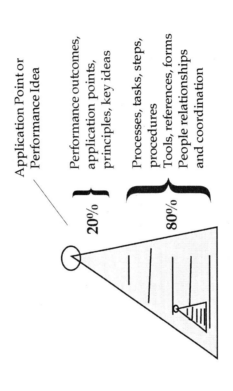

Application Point or Performance Idea

20% { Performance outcomes, application points, principles, key ideas

80% { Processes, tasks, steps, procedures
Tools, references, forms
People relationships and coordination

"Application Point" Pyramid

3-Minute e-Learning   *Subject Matter Expert (SME) Interview Guide*

SME Discovery Process

1 Preparations

A. Research what are business drivers, reasons, and issues around your content. What are current concerns that push the need for this program? What has to be changed in the content area? How does this topic impact organizational issues, benefits, costs, strategies, etc.?

B. Review current or previous training on this area.

C. Obtain an outline or content of the program.

D. Learn about the SMEs in advance: the nature and scope of his/her expertise, his style, role, and training background.

E. Arrange for a meeting. If needed, arrange an initial meeting with the content sponsor, end-user, leader, or stakeholder to ascertain the desired outcomes. In this initial meeting, ask questions in #1 above.

After this first step, arrange for a one-one-meeting with the SME.

2 Meeting the SME

A. State upfront your research findings, i.e. mission, goals, and outcomes from #1, specially the inputs of the champions and stakeholders.

B. Clarify that there are e-learning programs that qualify or do not qualify for a rapid development; discuss the flow chart of the "Application Point" Pyramid, its costs, speed and design approach. Get an agreement if the process is acceptable or how it can be modified. Get agreement on the review and approval process (see item E below.)

C. Interview the SME using SME questionnaire. If you wish the SME to input the information and content, provide the SME with the form, template, or software access.

D. Agree to submit a "granular lesson" model or mock-up for the SMEs' review. It is best to provide a working e-Learning prototype for the model.

E. Facilitate the process of approval and review by using a Content Layout template or software and a collaboration

3 Development Process

A. Develop, sell and train your team to ensure your they follow a process.

B. Use reusable templates, models, prototypes and processes.

C. Present to SMEs and your team an agreed upon library of interactive designs, lesson layout, image designs and approaches, writing style, different "Organics" models for easy use, reference and consistency. The more consistent your team is the easier it is to work with SMEs.

D. Package your design in terms of budget, cost, timeline impacts and communicate these with internal clients and SMEs. This helps create impact on their expectations in content presentation and the consequence to rapid development.

3-Minute e-Learning   Subject Matter Expert (SME) Interview Guide
SME Interview Guide and Form

1 Main Pages

What are the performance outcomes? What problems are we trying to solve? What opportunities are we trying to exploit? What are critical few key ideas we need to convey? What are positive and negative consequences if we fail to apply the critical ideas? What is a good real-life case, example, story, scenario, model, metaphor, etc. that learners can relate to? If you draw an image or picture, what would that be?

2 Jump Pages

What specific information do you wish to highlight in this detailed link page? What should the learner be looking for to better understand the performance areas?

3 Link Pages

What are detailed references, tools, processes, steps, checklists, court case, legislation, policies, etc. that you wish the learner to know?

4 Review Page(s)
Link Pages

What questions, reflections, activity, case, idea, phrase, etc. can help the learner reflect and ponder on the performance outcomes? What suggestions can you provide to see how the learners may apply these ideas in their work?

5 Assessment/Test Questions.

As an option and if needed for compliance, what test questions will you ask to gauge if the learner has read, retained, understood, "click the page", etc.

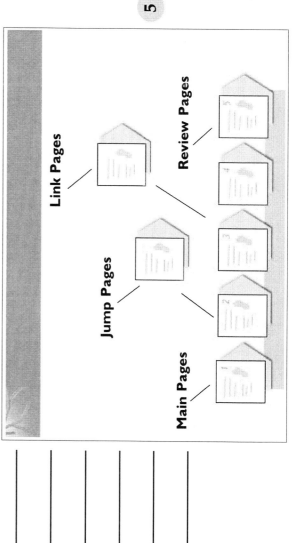

Link Pages

Jump Pages

Review Pages

Main Pages

3-Minute e-Learning   *Subject Matter Expert (SME) Interview Guide*

SME Interview Form / Granular Level

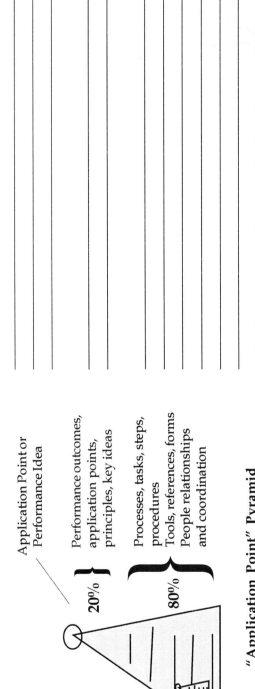

Application Point or
Performance Idea

} 20%

Performance outcomes,
application points,
principles, key ideas

} 80%

Processes, tasks, steps,
procedures
Tools, references, forms
People relationships
and coordination

"Application Point" Pyramid

3-Minute e-Learning
Bibliography

Bibliography

Research foundations in the formulation of assumptions and practices reported in this book.

Aldrich, C. (2004). *Simulations and The Future of Learning.* Pfeiffer

Laurel, B. (1993). *Computers as Theater.* Addison-Wesley Publishing Company

Bersin, J. (2006). *The High Impact Learning Organization.* Bersin & Associates

Brown, J.S. & Duguid, P. (200). *The Social Life of Information.* Harvard Business School Press

Brown, J.S., Denning, S., Groh, K., & Prusak, L. (2004). *Storytelling in Organizations.* Harvard Business Press

Cross, J. & Dublin, L. (2002). *Implementing e-Learning.* ASTD

Cross, J. (2006). *Informal Learning: Rediscovering the Natural Pathways That Inspire Innovation and Performance.* Pfeiffer

Cross, R. (2004). *The Hidden Power of Social Networks: Understanding How Work Really Gets Done in Organizations.* Harvard Business School Publishing Press

DiDonato, J. (2006) *Workforce Performance 2006 Conference: Searchable Wizards, Federated Search, Embedded Training.* White Papers

Gery, G. (1991) *Electronic Performance Support System.* Gery Associates

Malone, T. (2005). *The Future of Work: How the New Order of Business Will Shape Your Organization, Your Management Style and Your Life.* Harvard Business School Press

Masie, E. March 21, 2006. *18 Wishes for an LMS*
http://trends.masie.com/archives/2006/03/385_18_wishes_f.html

Masie, E. (2004). *Learning Rants, Raves, and Reflections: A Collection of Passionate and Professional Perspectives.* Pfeiffer

Postman, N. (1992). *Technopoly.* Vintage Books

Quartz, S. & Sejnowski, T. (2002). *Liars, Lovers and Heroes: What the New Brain Science Reveals About How We Become Who We Are.* Harper Collins

Rosenberg, M. (2005). *Beyond e-Learning: Approaches and Technologies to Enhance Organizational Knowledge, Learning, and Performance.* Pfeiffer

Schank, R. (2002). *Designing World-Class e-Learning How IBM, GE, Harvard Business School, and Columbia University are succeeding at e-Learning.* McGraw-Hill

Schank, R. (1990). *Tell Me a Story: Narrative and Intelligence.* Northwestern University Press, 1990

Van Dam, N. (2004) *The e-Learning Fieldbook: Implementation Lessons and Case Studies from Companies that are Making E-Learning Work.* McGraw-Hill

Vanthournout, D., et al. (2006). *Return on Learning.* Agate Publishing

Calhoun, W., Pollock, R., Jefferson, A. & Flanagan, R. (2006). *The Six Disciplines of Breakthrough Learning.* Pfeiffer

3-Minute e-Learning

Index

Index